# Why Be Catholic?

## TEN ANSWERS TO A
## VERY IMPORTANT QUESTION

### PATRICK MADRID

Foreword by Cardinal Seán O'Malley

IMAGE
New York

Published in the United States by Image, an imprint of the
Crown Publishing Group, a division of Random House LLC,
a Penguin Random House Company, New York.
www.crownpublishing.com

IMAGE is a registered trademark and the "I" colophon is a
trademark of Random House LLC.

Library of Congress Cataloging-in-Publication Data is available upon request.

ISBN 978-0-307-98643-6
eBook ISBN 978-0-307-98644-3

Printed in the United States of America

Book design by Helene Berinsky
Cover design by Nupoor Gordon
Cover photograph: Nagel Photography/Shutterstock
Author photograph: Nancy Madrid

10 9 8 7 6 5 4 3 2 1

First Edition

*To my parents, Bernard and Gretchen Madrid, who gave me the two greatest gifts of all, life and the Catholic faith*

# Contents

# Foreword

When I was Bishop of the U.S. Virgin Islands, my friends at Catholic Extension recommended Catholic Answers to me, because we were facing some very aggressive proselytizing on the part of some fundamentalist churches. Father Edward Slattery, now Bishop Slattery of Tulsa, told me about Karl Keating, a lawyer from California who started Catholic Answers to defend and explain our Catholic faith. He encouraged me to invite Karl to come to the Virgin Islands for an apologetics tour, and he offered to underwrite the expenses of hosting that event.

When I contacted Karl he said that he wasn't available, but he offered to send one of his best speakers, Patrick Madrid. Because Patrick is bilingual, it was a twofer—since he would be able to give conferences in both English and in Spanish. Patrick asked me to publicize his lectures as "open to the public" and to invite Catholics, fundamentalists, and anyone else who might be interested to our cathedral to hear him speak. I was so nervous, I removed the Blessed

Sacrament, expecting the worst! But I need not have worried. Patrick gave an extraordinary exposition of the Catholic faith, thoroughly based in Scripture. I realized that many of our Catholics were beginning to look at the Bible as the *enemy book*. But now, suddenly, they could see that it is the Word of God and is *our book*. Patrick answered their questions brilliantly and very respectfully. He understood how to defuse people's anger and fear. When I was greeting the people at the door following the presentation, all of the Catholics asked, "When is this man coming again?" And some of the fundamentalists asked, "How can I become a Catholic?"

From St. Thomas, we went to St. Croix, where we had a large outdoor rally with hundreds of people. One lady handed Patrick a booklet she received from the fundamentalists who visited her home many times, and she asked for a comment on what they said about the pope. The book displayed a sketch of the papal tiara, and on it was an inscription in Latin: *Vicarius Filii Dei*. The commentary said that if you took all of the letters from that inscription that are Roman numerals and added up their numerical value you would find it equaled six hundred sixty-six, which, as it says in Revelation 13:15–18, is the satanic number of the Beast. Patrick wrote all of this on the board and demonstrated that in fact it was true. However, he went on to explain that "Vicar of the Son of God" has never been an official title of the pope, much less his "name." One of the pope's official titles is "Vicar of Christ," but never "Vicar of the Son of God." Patrick then asked the crowd if anyone knew the name of the founder of the organization that had published that anti-Catholic propaganda. Several people shouted out the name. Patrick wrote it on the blackboard, extracted the letters that were Roman numerals, and added up their numerical value. It was 666! A cheer went up from the crowd. Needless to say, the Church is very lucky to have apologists like Patrick Madrid, who are so competent and so respectful, and who have such a deep sense of mission.

The Church needs apologists like Patrick Madrid, and we all need resources such as this book, *Why Be Catholic?* It helps to remind us all of what the Church stands for, what she teaches, and most of all how she is called to be a place of welcome and hope. As much as we have suffered these past few years in the Church because of the sins of a few, there is also reason to have hope and to cling to Christ, the Head of the Body, which is the Church. I pray that all who read this book will discover in it a rich source of faith and clarity, especially for those who are thinking of becoming Catholic. You are most welcome!

Our challenge in the New Evangelization is to transform secularized Christians into apostles and inviters, reaching out to the people of today to offer them answers to the questions they have in their hearts and to help them find a path that leads to God through a life of discipleship in the Catholic Church. Our first task is to introduce people to Christ, to His Love and Mercy, and to His presence in our lives.

Many people have written the Catholic Church off as simply a player in the cultural wars, but in reality the

Church's message is that of Christ, and He is the answer to the deepest longings of the human heart. One of the reasons that Pope Francis's message is making such a sensation in the world is that it is forcing people again to focus on the merciful face of God, reaching out to sinners and the suffering. In the pages that follow, Patrick Madrid opens our eyes to see the Church as the place where God's face is revealed, His mercy is received, and His love is shared.

—Cardinal Seán O'Malley, O.F.M., Cap.

November 2013

feasance and similar delinquencies on the part of priests and bishops has made the situation even more intolerable.

The grave effects of these scandals, in particular the sexual ones, are incalculable. First and foremost, of course, is the tragic toll taken on the innocent victims who were devastated by the crimes committed against them. As we now know, some Catholic bishops, who were in authority over these men, stonewalled, covered up, and hid behind weasel-word pretexts about how they were "just following the advice of the mental-health professionals" who assured them that it was A-okay to allow offenders back into parish ministry, in contact again with children.

The Archdiocese of Boston became "Ground Zero" for the eruption of the priest sex scandals in the United States. It was there, in 2002, that five Catholic clergymen were arrested, charged, and eventually imprisoned for their depredations against adolescents and children. No one realized then just how far the rot extended.

In his sermon preached at his 2003 installation Mass, the new Archbishop of Boston, Seán Patrick O'Malley, O.F.M., Cap., addressed this crisis head-on:

> The whole Catholic community is ashamed and anguished because of the pain and the damage inflicted on so many young people, and because of our inability or unwillingness to deal with the crime of sexual abuse of minors. To those victims and to their families, we beg forgiveness and we assure them that the Catholic Church is working to create a safe environment for young people. It must never be business as usual, but

rather a firm commitment on the part of every diocese, parish, and school to do all we can to avoid the mistakes of the past and create safeguards for the future. . . . How, ultimately, we deal with this present crisis in our Church will do much to define us as Catholics of the future. We must not flee from the cross of pain and humiliation. If we stand firm in who we are, in what we believe, if we work together—hierarchy, clergy, religious, laity—to live our faith and fulfill our mission, then we will be a stronger and a holier Church. This should be of some consolation to those victims who have opened old wounds in their hearts by coming forward. Your pain will not be in vain. Our Church and our nation will become a safer place for children.[2]

There is no way to undo the horrendous damage done to the victims of these scandals. The general goodwill, respect, and trust that had previously been extended toward the Catholic Church have now largely evaporated. The scandals have fueled an increasingly cynical attitude toward Catholics that at times rises to the level of active hostility. Several faithful and virtuous Catholic priests I know personally have confided to me their own shock, embarrassment, and discouragement at having been the innocent targets of animosity from total strangers in public places. One described how, in an airport terminal, he sat down on a chair across from a young mother and her child. When the woman looked up and saw him, she pulled the toddler close to her, glared at the priest, and hissed loudly enough for everyone around to hear, "You stay away from my child!"

Gathering the child into her arms, she stalked off, leaving him stunned and humiliated. This man had done nothing to violate his vows, but thanks to the Judas priests who *did* betray them so grotesquely, he and many other good and innocent priests have become "collateral damage."

So, considering the enormous black cloud hanging over the Catholic Church, society's increasingly cynical and hostile attitude toward the Church, and the fact that fewer and fewer Catholics devoutly practice the faith, why would anyone in his right mind write a book whose purpose is to encourage people to *become* Catholic? Acknowledging the tragic reality of scandals in the Catholic Church is the only appropriate first step toward providing an adequate and meaningful context (not excuses)to show that, in spite of these scandals, there remains a solid and compelling case for why people should be Catholic. Because I believe a solid foundation for Catholicism remains beneath the phenomenon of disgusting Church scandals, through analysis I will provide context (not excuses) to show that this is the case.

In spite of the scandals, the Catholic Church has the answer to all of life's most urgent problems and challenges. In fact, the very fact that we are justifiably shocked and horrified by terrible deeds done by Catholics underscores what happens when Catholic moral teachings, for example, are ignored and contravened, *especially* by clergy, given the general perception that these men have in some sense been "called to a higher, stricter standard of behavior."

The Catholic Church's answer to the myriad of life's problems we all must face in some form or another is simply the gospel of Jesus Christ. It is the Catholic Church's response to the world's easy, glittery enticements to pursue a life of unfettered pleasure, power, and pride. These carnal enticements the Holy Bible refers to as the "world, the flesh, and the devil":

> [Y]ou were dead through the trespasses and sins in which you once walked, following the course of this world, following the prince of the power of the air, the spirit that is now at work in the sons of disobedience. Among these we all once lived in the passions of our flesh, following the desires of body and mind, and so we were by nature children of wrath, like the rest of mankind. (Eph. 2:1–3)

The Catholic Church speaks the words of the Lord Jesus Christ in response to the glitzy blandishments of the world:

> And behold, one came up to him, saying, "Teacher, what good deed must I do, to have eternal life?" And he said to him, "Why do you ask me about what is good? One there is who is good. If you would enter life, keep the commandments." He said to him, "Which?" And Jesus said, "You shall not kill, You shall not commit adultery, You shall not steal, You shall not bear false witness, Honor your father and mother, and, You shall love your neighbor as yourself." The young man said to him, "All these I have observed; what do I still lack?" Jesus said to him, "If you would be perfect, go, sell what you possess and give to the poor, and you will have treasure in heaven; and come, follow me." When

the young man heard this he went away sorrowful; for he had great possessions. And Jesus said to his disciples, "Truly, I say to you, it will be hard for a rich man to enter the kingdom of heaven. Again I tell you, it is easier for a camel to go through the eye of a needle than for a rich man to enter the kingdom of God." When the disciples heard this they were greatly astonished, saying, "Who then can be saved?" But Jesus looked at them and said to them, "With men this is impossible, but with God all things are possible." (Matt. 19:16–26)

Many times, I've imagined myself as that young man. How would I have responded to Jesus? What would I have done with my wealth? I know from experience, as I'm sure you do, how powerful the lure of worldly things and attitudes and appetites can be, and I look back, as I'm sure you do, with a certain measure of sorrow and regret for the times when I gave in to them.

The Catholic Church itself is the ark of salvation, because the head of the Church is Christ, not its sinful members. And there have always been and always will be times when it appears that he is asleep when the wind and waves of life toss the Church so violently that it seems it will founder and sink. "Teacher, do you not care if we perish?" his apostles asked him during a storm when he was asleep on a cushion (Mark 4:38). Christ arose and calmed the wind and the waves and then said to them, "Why are you so afraid? Have you no faith?"

I can say that I have faith in Christ and in his promises to be with the Church always, no matter what, no matter how bad some of the members of the Church may be. The measure by which one should rightly judge the Catholic Church, at least on historical grounds, cannot be reduced merely to a weighing up of the sum total of good and bad deeds performed by Catholics. After all, Jesus himself described the Church's circumstances as being situated in a "field of wheat and weeds":

> The kingdom of heaven may be compared to a man who sowed good seed in his field; but while men were sleeping, his enemy came and sowed weeds among the wheat, and went away. So when the plants came up and bore grain, then the weeds appeared also. And the servants of the householder came and said to him, "Sir, did you not sow good seed in your field? How then has it weeds?" He said to them, "An enemy has done this." The servants said to him, "Then do you want us to go and gather them?" But he said, "No; lest in gathering the weeds you root up the wheat along with them. Let both grow together until the harvest; and at harvest time I will tell the reapers, Gather the weeds first and bind them in bundles to be burned, but gather the wheat into my barn." (Matt. 13:24–30)

Christ then explains the meaning of this parable:

> Then he left the crowds and went into the house. And his disciples came to him, saying, "Explain to us the parable of the weeds of the field." He answered, "He who sows the good seed is the Son of man; the field

is the world, and the good seed means the sons of the kingdom; the weeds are the sons of the evil one, and the enemy who sowed them is the devil; the harvest is the close of the age, and the reapers are angels. Just as the weeds are gathered and burned with fire, so will it be at the close of the age. The Son of man will send his angels, and they will gather out of his kingdom all causes of sin and all evildoers, and throw them into the furnace of fire; there men will weep and gnash their teeth. Then the righteous will shine like the sun in the kingdom of their Father. He who has ears, let him hear." (Matt. 13:36–43)

The uncomfortable and even confusing circumstances his Church would perennially find itself in could be likened to a "field of wheat and weeds," the field being the world and the wheat and weeds being analogous to good and bad Christians (i.e., those who are his genuine followers and those who simply have an outward appearance of fidelity to him). In other words, according to Christ's own will, the Church has always existed in a state of weeds among the wheat. One subtlety in this parable is that the weeds (tare, darnel) look nearly identical to wheat, making them practically indistinguishable from each other. In fact, as any wheat farmer will tell you, it is very difficult for the untrained eye to tell them apart, and it would therefore be quite easy to mistakenly tear up the good wheat along with the weeds. One other important little detail is that the head of the darnel weed stands straight up, not unlike stiff-necked Christians who are proud of their virtue (see the story of the Pharisee and the poor Publican in Luke 18:9–14 for a refresher on this), while the head of wheat droops slightly, reminiscent of true humility.

Why did Christ arrange things such that the Church would always be populated by great sinners as well as great saints and everyone in between? I don't know why, but this unlikely game plan has always been the case. Let's consider a few lowlights from the hit parade of scandals that snakes its way through the biblical narrative.

At the very beginning of human history, the diabolical Serpent slithered into Adam and Eve's pristine Garden. Rather than laugh and spurn his devilish wheedling, they fell for his lies, disobeyed God, and forfeited (for themselves and for the rest of us) eternal life and liberty, and found themselves naked and ashamed and stumbling in a now-confused pursuit of happiness (Gen. 3).

After heroically believing in God, building the Ark, and saving his family and a whole bunch of animals from the Flood, Noah, a righteous man, went on a wine bender and got totally wasted (Gen. 9:20 v. 24.).[3]

Abraham, the great patriarch, duplicitously pretended that his drop-dead gorgeous wife, Sarah, was his *sister* (she was his niece), so as to avoid being hassled by the Egyptians when the couple was sojourning in that land. His scheme got so out of hand that Pharaoh, believing that Sarah was single, planned to marry her before he found out that she was married (Gen. 12:10–20). Some years later, after they had left Egypt, a still-childless Sarah convinced her husband to sleep with their maid, Hagar. Abraham complied and fathered a child with her. Eventually, when Sarah and

Abraham had a child of their own together, she became jealous of Ishmael, the bastard son of Hagar, and she angrily drove mother and son out into the desert wilderness to die (Gen. 16).[4]

Joseph's brothers, jealous of their father's special love for him, threw him down a dry well and, while they ate lunch, tried to concoct a lie to tell their father by way of explaining why Joseph had gone missing. When a band of merchants passed by, they hoisted Joseph back up and sold him to the traders. Then, going to their father, they lied and said Joseph had been killed by a wild animal (Gen. 37). Some brothers!

Don't even get me started on the scandals found in books 1 and 2 of Samuel. You want murder, adultery, rape, violence, greed, intrigues, and pride? Look no further. King David, whom God called "a man after my own heart," got so caught up in lust for Bathsheba, another man's wife, that he seduced and impregnated her and then had her husband conveniently bumped off in battle. He was an adulterer *and* a murderer. And yet, God's grace was more powerful than David's sins and, when he repented, God restored him and made mighty use of him, in spite of his sins and weaknesses.

David's Psalm 51 is one of the most poignant and moving examples of repentance and forgiveness, even amid terrible scandals:

> *Have mercy on me, O God, according to thy steadfast love;*
> *according to thy abundant mercy blot out my transgressions.*

*Wash me thoroughly from my iniquity,*
*and cleanse me from my sin!*

*For I know my transgressions,*
*and my sin is ever before me.*
*Against thee, thee only, have I sinned,*
*and done that which is evil in thy sight,*
*so that thou art justified in thy sentence*
*and blameless in thy judgment. (Ps. 51:1–4)*

Even in the New Testament we see scandals. Astonishingly, even Christ's own handpicked men were the source of scandal. The worst of all was Judas, who betrayed the Lord for thirty pieces of silver. Peter denied him three times, once under oath; all the other apostles (with the exception of John) abandoned him and fled in fear.

Some Catholics don't grow as wheat but as weeds, causing damage to those around them, for example, the clerical sex abuse scandals. What is needed is an honest and forthright discussion of the terrible crimes committed by the priests who molested children and the bishops who covered up their crimes, shuffled them around to unsuspecting parishes, and failed to protect their flock. This deplorable reality is not in itself a disproof of the divine mission of the Catholic Church; rather, it is a reminder of why Catholics should be humble, and it is proof that without God's grace and a sincere commitment on our part to avoid evil and do good, anyone can fall into gross sin.

Examples of such dark chapters in Catholic history could be multiplied, of course, and so often this is exactly what the Church's critics seek to do ad nauseam, sometimes to the point of fantastically exaggerating them. Yet these critics often ignore the innumerable good Catholics seeking to be humble, virtuous, and attentive to helping others. And, of course, there are the courageous acts of Catholic men and women who give everything they have, sometimes including their own lives, for the sake of helping other people. The spectacular sins get all the attention and the great good works and holiness that characterize many other Catholics go largely unnoticed—and that is not a bad thing. A discussion of what Jesus meant in two passages: Matthew 5 ("You are the light of the world. . . . Let your light so shine before men . . .") and Luke 17:1 ("Scandals will come, but woe to him by whom they come"). The Catholic Church mirrors the mix of good and bad in Christ's own handpicked apostles.

Scandals are part of the life of the Church not *because* of its teachings and customs, but because individual Catholics choose to reject and ignore those teachings. For example, the ancient Catholic custom of priestly celibacy, freely chosen by men "for the sake of the kingdom" (Matt. 19:10–12), is not the cause of sexual misbehavior among priests. It is when a priest *abandons* his commitment to striving for the ideal that he backslides into sin.

When one approaches history with premeditated negative assumptions, prejudices, and hostility toward a particular group of people, it can be exceedingly difficult, if not impossible, to correctly understand why they fail. The fact is, society *expects* Catholics to live up to the high moral standards imposed by Catholic teaching, and it is shocking when a priest or a bishop betrays his solemn promise to be a chaste celibate.

Why do we see so many examples of bad Catholics? A widespread error has infected many Catholics with the notion that "as long as I don't kill someone, as long as I'm a 'good person' and am not doing anything seriously wrong, I'm okay and on my way to heaven." This "I'm okay, you're okay" cult of comfortable self-contentment has effectively driven out of many people's minds the realization that the Good News of Jesus Christ is one of repentance, turning from sin, forgiveness, and salvation.

Consider a few examples of Christ's teaching on this point:

- "I tell you . . . unless you repent, you will all likewise perish" (Luke 13:3).
- "He who does not take his cross and follow me is not worthy of me" (Matt. 10:38).
- "Not every one who says to me, 'Lord, Lord,' shall enter the kingdom of heaven, but he who does the will of my Father who is in heaven. On that day many will say to me, 'Lord, Lord, did we not prophesy in your name, and cast out demons in your name, and do many mighty works in your name?' And then will I declare to them, 'I never knew you; depart from me, you evildoers.' Every one then who hears these words of mine and does them will be like a wise man who built his house upon the rock; and the rain fell, and the floods came, and the winds blew and beat upon that house, but it did not fall, because it had been

founded on the rock. And every one who hears these words of mine and does not do them will be like a foolish man who built his house upon the sand; and the rain fell, and the floods came, and the winds blew and beat against that house, and it fell; and great was the fall of it." (Matt. 7:21–27)

Scandal, like the vices that spawn it, can only be combated by virtue. For example, to root out the sin of lust, cultivate its opposing virtue: chastity. To eradicate pride, cultivate humility; anger must be balanced by patience. The single greatest danger to the Christian life, the enemy of grace, is not the devil or his temptations; it's not the world or the flesh; it is complacency, what the Bible calls "lukewarmness."

Jesus declared: "I know your works: you are neither cold nor hot. Would that you were cold or hot! So, because you are lukewarm, and neither cold nor hot, I will spew you out of my mouth" (Rev. 3:15–16). What termites are to a wooden structure, lukewarmness is to a Christian. Termites work out of sight, out of mind, continuously gnawing away at the timbers until one day, without its owner ever realizing just how deteriorated the structure had become, the house collapses in on itself. In the same way, complacency weakens a person gradually but steadily and, if left unchecked, results in a total moral collapse.

The causes of scandal are all traceable to that one decisive choice to say "yes" to serious sin, one that is usually the result of a whole series of imperceptible little affirmations and compromises with sin. Scandals start when someone makes a decision to take the easy path, the option that is front-loaded with pleasure.

We all know that the devil is the enemy of God and therefore he is our enemy. It drives the devil crazy when human beings strive to be virtuous, because that is a sure sign that they are not under his influence and are headed toward heaven. So, it doesn't take a genius to figure out that the devil will make use of any tools within his reach to derail someone's progress toward the Lord by distracting him with pleasurable trifles, whispering in his ear (just as he did to Eve way back in the Garden) that it's really no big deal to cut this one little corner, just this once. Everyone else does it, after all, and besides, God will forgive him. Go ahead! Enjoy this little delight. God doesn't really care about little things, especially when there are so many really wicked people out there. Go ahead. Come on in! The water's fine! What have you got to lose?

Oh yes, the devil *delights* in scandals. He wants us to compromise and cut corners, just a little here and there is fine, at least at first. But the more we compromise, the more he can maneuver us into just the right precarious position the better to topple us into the abyss of sin hardly without our even being aware of what's happening.

Picture Noah's neighbors the day the rain started. "Eh, just a little drizzle," they thought to themselves. "No big deal." Yet the rain persisted. When it started pooling up around their ankles, some started feeling uneasy but shrugged it off, thinking, "Hey, we've had downpours before. No problemo. This'll clear up soon enough." But by the time they were clambering up onto the roof to escape the raging waters, well, that's when stone-cold panic set in. But by then, it was too late.

> As were the days of Noah, so will be the coming of the Son of man. For as in those days before the flood they were eating and drinking, marrying and giving in marriage, until the day when Noah entered the ark, and they did not know until the flood came and swept them all away. (Matt. 24:37–39)

This is how sin works. It typically creeps up on you, imperceptibly at first, like a cat stalking a bird. Slowly, quietly, *patiently*. And then, BOOM! It's got you. Acquiescence in little things leads to acquiescence in bigger things. "Oh, it's just a pack of chewing gum," the teenager reassures herself as she shoplifts, "no one will miss it." Later, after enough time of suppressing the truth by ignoring her guilty conscience with these easy rationalizations, she effortlessly coasts into stealing more expensive things. Eventually, she's doing time in prison for felony theft and need only look back on her life's pattern of saying "yes" to seemingly insignificant sins and how each of them "greased the skids," so to speak, enabling her to slide further down this slippery slope toward worse things. In due course, this downward trajectory carries her right into a jail cell.

The voice of our conscience warns us against doing things we know deep down are bad and wrong, and, after we've done them, it reminds us of our guilt and also prods us to repent and turn away from sin. This is true for everyone, everywhere. It is a universal human condition, because our innate awareness of good and evil and that we should do what is good and avoid doing what is evil is written on our hearts. In other words, God hardwired us for virtue and moral integrity. Serious sin is like a rogue electrical surge, a voltage spike of passion or malice that will thoroughly fry the circuits of your soul if you give in to it.

The Catholic Church offers the solution to the problem of sin—a divinely designed surge protector of truth—in its moral teachings. To use a different analogy, Catholic moral teachings are akin to flashing lights and warning signs on a highway (Bridge Out! Slow Down! Flooding Ahead! Turn Around—Don't Drown!), and its sacraments repair and restore the damage we inflict on ourselves when we don't heed those warning signs and get ourselves into everything from fender-benders to high-speed, head-on collisions.

This is why I am Catholic and why you should be, too. The Catholic Church, with all its problems and sinful members, teaches the truth that will set us free, even though not every Catholic obeys those teachings. Perhaps, in a strange way, we can see in the terrible spate of scandals a kind of "negative proof" that the Catholic Church really *is* that Noah's Ark of salvation that Christ invites us to board. For it is precisely when Catholics (like the priests and bishops who participated in and/or covered up those sexual crimes) ignore and disobey Catholic moral teaching that we are so justifiably horrified. They didn't live up to the high moral standards that Christ calls us to. They are like passengers on the Ark who abandon ship and dive overboard to go body surfing. And you see where it gets them. Those who stay on board the Ark may have to endure cramped, smelly, and sometimes frustrating conditions, but they will be saved in the end.

## 2

# You *Can* Handle the Truth

### The Historical Case for
### the Catholic Church

✠ IN MY OWN SEARCH FOR ANSWERS TO THE QUESTION *Why be Catholic?*, I determined early on that having a good feeling about the Catholic Church was no substitute for knowing whether or not the teachings of the Catholic Church are true. For me, plausibility was not enough. I needed to know whether these teachings were, in fact, true. If they weren't, I wanted no part of the Catholic Church. In fact, if even *some* Catholic teachings were false, I told myself, I'd hit the door running and never look back.

When I was a child, my rationale for being Catholic was simple: "My parents said it. I believe it. That settles it." I had, as we all did at one time, a childlike faith. But as I grew older it gradually became clear to me that being Catholic and accepting Catholic teaching just because that's what my parents told me was not enough of a reason. The older I got, and the more life's rich pageant of tantalizing discoveries and experiences impressed themselves on my mind, the more I came to see that I had to test these teachings to see whether they held up under scrutiny. I discovered that not only were there lots of non-Catholics out there, but more than a few of them did not like the Catholic Church.

When I was eleven, I got into a chance discussion about God with an atheist lady who lived across the street. Once, while she was driving my sister and me somewhere as a favor for our mom, I happened to mention God in an otherwise innocuous conversation. This set her off, and she proceeded to berate me. "There is no such thing as God," she scolded. "He doesn't exist, and people who believe in 'God' believe in a myth." Needless to say, at eleven years old, I was pretty defenseless against her atheist sloganeering about how God doesn't exist. I can't remember anything about what arguments she used, although I do recall not finding them persuasive.

When I was fourteen, a pair of earnest Mormon missionaries showed up at our front door. They were nice enough at first, and when I invited them in and we sat in the living room, I kind of liked the fact that two nineteen-year-olds would have an interest in talking on a serious level with someone my age. But as soon as the conversation ventured into the tenets of Mormonism, I got fired up and began arguing with them. They could quote Bible passages freely and I couldn't. I knew that what these two Mormon guys were telling me wasn't right, but I didn't have enough knowledge to explain *why*. I felt my curiosity being piqued in a new way. I wanted to dig deeper into my own Catholic faith, its history and doctrines, so that I could more effectively discuss it the next time missionaries showed up.

I gradually began bumping into more difficult and challenging arguments against my Catholic faith. Some came from Protestants, Mormons, and Jehovah's Witnesses, others from Muslims, Jews, Hindus, other non-Christians, and atheists. Each in his own way, and with his own set of objections, challenged my Catholic beliefs using the Bible, historical events (real and imagined), logical arguments (and some illogical ones), claims to revelations that were incompatible with the claims of Jesus Christ, science, and the dull yet forceful arguments against God's existence. Plenty of atheists, too, have taken their fair share of whacks at my belief in God over the years.

My theory is that most people who have lived enough life have a "golden summer" somewhere in their past. By this I mean a fondly remembered stretch of time redolent of happiness, satisfaction, and genial experiences and relationships.

Mine was the summer of 1977. It was all the more golden because I was dating a pretty blonde Protestant girl named Christie. When I asked her out on a date, she said, "yes," but insisted that I first must come to her home and meet her parents. No problem, I thought. I'm sure they'll like me.

As it happened, her parents did like me, and I enjoyed being around them too, which was a bonus. But as Christie confided to me early on, her mom and dad were not at all keen on the fact that I was Catholic. My guess is that they tolerated me dating their daughter, but I'm sure they would have preferred it if Christie were seeing a Protestant guy, rather than a Catholic. They were sincere, warm, friendly, and fun to be around, and they showed me by their words and attitudes that they were deeply committed Christians, though not weirdly so—just normal, happy, Protestant folk. This had a lot to do with why I spent so much time at Christie's house that summer—that and the fact that they also had a built-in swimming pool, which definitely sweetened the deal.

In spite of all the fun I was having with Christie and her family, I soon sensed that her dad saw me as a kind of "project."

Before swimming in their pool or hopping in the car with Christie to go get pizza or see a movie, her father would invariably ask me first to sit down with him in their living room, where he'd then break out his large, well-worn King James Bible and begin asking me pointed questions about various Catholic beliefs and practices. I, of course, did not have a Bible with me. I had one at home, though. A beautiful, leather-bound, personally inscribed gift Bible that my confirmation sponsor had given me, but I didn't read it very often and, as a result, I didn't know anywhere near as much as Christie's dad did about what was in it.

What followed was a ten- or fifteen-minute discourse in which Christie's dad explained in his friendly, patient way why the "*Roman* Catholic Church" was wrong about this, that, and the other doctrine or practice: "call no man father," the authority of the pope, the notion that Catholics think they can "earn" their salvation, confession to a priest, infant baptism, purgatory, and, of course, Mary. He hammered me pretty hard on all of these issues. That summer, I found out the hard way that Catholic teaching on Mary was a major issue for Christie's dad. The Immaculate Conception, honoring and praying to Mary, and her perpetual virginity were all issues about which he treated me to vigorous biblical arguments.

Happily, my parents' large library of good Catholic books in our home meant I didn't have to look very far for the answers to the questions Christie's dad had been raising. One particularly helpful set of apologetic books was the three-volume set of *Radio Replies*, which answered literally hundreds of common challenges against the Catholic Church, not just from Protestants but from atheists as well. It proved to be a gold mine of information! Even though the *Radio Replies* series was at least forty years old, the crisp, concise, and compelling answers it gave were exactly what I needed to help me counter Christie's dad's barrage of biblical and historical arguments. The more I researched the biblical and historical answers to these issues, the more I wanted to dig deeper. As each new challenge came my way and I took the time necessary to study and probe and find the answers, I became increasingly confident that the Catholic answers to these objections were compelling and convincing. The Catholic faith *itself,* on its own merits, had begun to persuade me—imperceptibly and without my fully realizing it. I was starting to lay hold of the solid, satisfying answers to the question that had loomed large in my mind all summer: *Why be Catholic?*

At this point, the tenor of my conversations with Christie's dad began to change. I became more assertive (respectfully, of course, as I didn't want to do anything to irk him into not allowing me to come around anymore), and he seemed to me to become more frustrated. He may have seen me at first as a helpless Catholic "fish" he could steadily "reel in" on the sturdy line of his biblical arguments against the *Roman* Catholic Church. But as the summer wore on, he had to work a good deal harder to turn the reel. By August 16, 1977, I knew I was the "fish that got away." That was the day Elvis Presley died. Christie and I were out for a walk around the neighborhood that sultry afternoon when a teenager we knew came out of her house and called to us, "Hey! They just said on the radio that Elvis is dead! Can you believe it?"

As improbable as it may seem, it was on that very day that it dawned on me that all the anti-Catholic arguments Christie's dad had challenged me with all summer, and all the "what if?" questions they had churned up in my mind, and all the opportunities those questions had offered me to start doubting (or disbelieving) my Catholic faith just didn't hold water. I began to see that though there might be tougher and ultimately unanswerable challenges I would have to confront somewhere down the road, at least for now, the "Death Cookie" and "call no man father" variety of arguments no longer held any sway over me. Like Elvis, they had died—suddenly and unexpectedly.

As an adult, I've been fortunate to meet and talk at length with Buddhists, Hindus, Muslims, Jews, and even a few Wiccans and other assorted self-professed "pagans." If for nothing else, I am grateful for each of these discussions because I learned a lot from these non-Christians about the tenets of their faiths and how I, as a Christian, could better explain my beliefs to them.

All of my research into Catholicism, from the time I was a teenager till the writing of this book, has led me to believe that Catholic history—the good, the bad, and the ugly—provides a compelling answer to the question *Why be Catholic?* Catholic history is messy, though—very messy, in fact. There have been some bad popes mingled in with the many good and even heroically great popes. There were countless brave martyrs for the Catholic faith who willingly gave up their lives rather than deny Christ during the period of ferocious Roman persecutions in the second through the third centuries. But there were also traitors, those who apostatized[1] at the first sign of trouble. None of the notorious subset of Catholic Crusaders, who committed terrible atrocities sometimes in the name of the Catholic Church and even of God Himself, can be excused or exonerated in any way.[2] Many ask, *How do I make sense of all these seemingly conflicting aspects of Catholic history?*

The two-thousand-year history of the Catholic Church is also suffused with great good works (establishing hospitals, orphanages, and other institutions to care for the poor) and selflessness (the countless monks, nuns, priests, and religious who devoted their lives to serving others). Catholic devotion to education is paramount: innumerable universities, colleges, and schools were founded to bring the light of reason and literacy to all people, regardless of their religion or skin color. The good deeds done by selfless Catholics do not, in and of themselves, prove the truth of the Catholic Church, though. Rather, these examples show the good that comes when people follow the teachings of the Catholic Church.

No matter how evil the actions of a given Catholic may be, and no matter how many examples of wicked Catholics one might point to, they don't in themselves prove anything beyond the fact that there are bad Catholics. In fact, they are evidence of what happens when one *disregards* and fails to live according to Catholic teaching. The Church is filled with an unending series of extremes: good and evil, saints and sinners, successes and failures, triumphs and disasters, strengths and weaknesses.

Though there is nowhere near enough space in this book to adequately plumb the depths of Catholic history, it is possible to accurately trace the outlines. Any global institution like the Catholic Church that has been in continuous existence for two millennia is going to have a tremendously rich, complex, and even problematic history that cannot be properly understood, much less appreciated, at a glance.

Understanding Christian history on its own terms became a passionate pursuit for me. I had always had a keen interest in reading books about Catholic antiquity, especially the lives of the saints, but the older I got, the more interested I became in studying the broader sweep of Catholic history, including those episodes involving Catholics who were anything but saints. The more I dug into the rich, fascinating, and sometimes startling details of Catholic history, the deeper I wanted to dig. The colorful and enigmatic cast of Catholic characters and the accounts of their roles in the vast drama of the Church's sojourn on earth deepened my hunger to know "the rest of the story."

Even those who are familiar with the basic outline of Christian history sometimes have a historical "blank spot" spanning the roughly fourteen hundred years that elapsed between the death of the last apostle, John, and 1517, when an Augustinian monk named Martin Luther burst onto the ecclesiastical scene and mobilized what would become the Protestant Reformation.

I've asked many people over the years, "What do you think happened in between the time of the apostles and the Protestant Reformation?"Answers vary. "The Dark Ages," some respond vaguely with a shrug and, apparently, not much interest in pursuing the matter further. Others say, "That's not important. What really matters is reading the Bible and believing in Jesus *now*, not what people said or did five hundred or a thousand years ago."

Luther and his bold, new theology, the ecclesiastical equivalent of the mythical Helen of Troy, launched not a thousand ships, but a thousand Protestant denominations.[3] The last five hundred years since Luther's rise to prominence have been marked by a seemingly endless fissioning of denominations. The original three major branches of the Continental protest movement against the Catholic Church—Lutheran, Calvinist, Anabaptist—were themselves the distinct theological groups that resulted from the first round of splintering shortly after Luther advanced his new theology. The "mainline" churches we know today have evolved from them, as did the Church of England, which arose in 1534 out of the ashes of King Henry VIII's acrimonious fracas with the pope over the latter's refusal to grant the monarch a divorce from his wife, resulting in Henry's fateful departure from the Catholic Church.[4]

In fact, the Catholic Church in the early sixteenth century was in dire need of reform. Unlike Saint Francis of Assisi, whose wise and brilliantly successful approach ultimately reformed a Church that had, in his day, fallen into shambles on many fronts, Martin Luther chose a path of rebellion that not only failed to reform the Church he once loved but inflicted a massive and still-suppurating wound of acrimonious division on the Body of Christ. This does not in any way excuse or minimize the enormous damage caused by those Catholics who were themselves responsible for the corruption. Nor is it an attempt to blame Luther for the corruption that he reacted so strenuously against.

At the Council of Trent, the Catholic Church did, in fact, undertake the urgently needed ecclesiastical reforms that Luther had identified. This Catholic Counter-Reformation was a big step forward in correcting the problems that had hampered and weakened the Church's mission of saving souls, but the damage had been done.

When I reflect on the Reformation, I take solace in knowing that, alone among all other Christian groups, the Catholic Church was always there, always on the scene, always present and accounted for, since the days of the apostles. What really caught my attention as I sifted through the details of Catholic history is something that I found impossible to explain away. In fact, I found it to be—for me, at least—an overwhelmingly convincing indication of the truth of the Catholic Church's claim to being *the* Church established by Jesus Christ.

It's rare these days to hear a Catholic make the claim that the Catholic Church is the one true Church established by Jesus Christ, even though that is the official belief of the Catholic Church, one that can be corroborated with compelling historical evidence. Rather, since the Second Vatican Council placed new emphasis on the importance of ecumenical dialogue with other Christian groups,[5] this Catholic teaching has faded considerably in the minds of many.[6] As result, many Catholics have at best a hazy sense of the great drama of Christianity spanning two millennia. They may know that Jesus and the apostles walked the dusty roads of Palestine some twenty centuries ago, and they know that there are Christians today, but what happened in between then and now is largely a blank to many.

If it can be demonstrated that Christ *did* establish the Catholic Church, then everyone on earth should be Catholic. I see this as the ultimate answer to the question *Why be Catholic?*

I found in the Gospel of Matthew a series of biblical clues leading me inexorably toward the conclusion that the Catholic Church is the one true Church. Each clue is but a strand in itself, but taken together, they form a stout rope of evidence that can more than heft the weight of the prodigious Catholic claim to being the Church that Christ established.

First: The Church Christ established is visible.

Jesus declares to his hearers: "You are the light of the world. A city set on a hill cannot be hid. Nor do men light a lamp and put it under a bushel, but on a stand, and it gives light to all in the house. Let your light so shine before men, that they may see your good works and give glory to your Father who is in heaven" (Matt. 5:14–16).

This statement has a twofold significance. First, it describes what each individual Christian is called to do and to be in this world: to shine forth to others the light of Christ.

Christ is also describing the Church he would establish as *visible*, not obscure or hidden. I asked myself: Why would Jesus have gone to all the trouble of establishing a Church just to make it so arcane and obscure that no one could ever really know for sure if he had found it? What good would that do?

Similarly, since Jesus never did things halfway or for no good reason, I asked myself what purpose it would serve for the Church he established to be hard to locate and how this would square with his statement that, individually and corporately, his followers, the Church, would stand out like a "city set on a hill." That sure seemed to me to be a promise that the Church would be clearly visible for those who were willing to look. And one additional realization deeply impressed itself on me, namely that Christ specifically ruled out the notion that his Church would be hard to locate when he said that no one "light[s] a lamp and put[s] it under a bushel," because doing so is counterproductive, self-defeating, and incoherent, and one thing is for certain: Jesus's own life and deeds show that he was none of those things. I don't think he could have been any clearer about this than when he said that the reason one would "light a lamp and put it . . . on a stand" is so that it can "give light to all in the house." This told me that the Church he established must also be prominent and visible.

Second: Jesus Christ, not some other man or woman, is the founder of his Church.

In Matthew 16:13–19, Jesus asks his apostles, "Who do men say that the Son of man is?" This elicits a series of incorrect answers: "Some say John the Baptist, others say Eli'jah, and others Jeremiah or one of the prophets."

Then, he asks the proverbial $64,000 question: "But who do *you* say that I am?"

Alone among the apostles, Simon Peter replies, "You are the Christ, the Son of the living God."

Jesus answers him, "Blessed are you, Simon Bar-Jona! For flesh and blood has not revealed this to you, but my Father who is in heaven. And I tell you, you are Peter, and on this rock I will build my church, and the powers of death shall not prevail against it. I will give you the keys of the kingdom of heaven, and whatever you bind on earth shall be bound in heaven, and whatever you loose on earth shall be loosed in heaven."

There is a great deal of important theological truth packed into this brief passage, and it's not my intention to explore that here, except to point out the particular line that sheds light on the Church the Lord was going to establish.

He says, "On this rock *I will build my church,* and the powers of death shall not prevail against it." This clue told me that, whichever Church it was, it had to be able to trace itself back in an unbroken line of continuity from the present day to Christ himself. Or to say it in a different way, any Church that was established by someone other than Christ could not credibly claim to be that Church. Some, such as Joseph Smith, the founder of the Church of Jesus Christ of Latter-day Saints (more commonly known as the Mormon Church), have claimed to have "restored" the true Church after it had been lost. A "Great Apostasy" destroyed the Church Christ established, they claim. But the biblical evidence refutes such a notion.

Third: Jesus promised that he would be with his Church "to the close of the age," or, to the end of the world (Matt. 28:19–20). This is another way of saying that the Church he established would last until the end, literally, come hell or high water.

The Catholic Church is "visible," both in its outward appearance of lay faithful, the pope, bishops, and priests, as well as in its distinctively Catholic doctrines, such as the Real Presence of Christ in the Eucharist, its Marian teachings, the Mass, purgatory, sacraments, and so forth. These clearly visible outward marks of the Catholic Church can be seen today. They can be seen two hundred years ago, five hundred years ago, a thousand years ago, fifteen hundred years ago. Indeed, they are visible and apparent some two thousand years ago, all the way back to the time of the apostles.

The Catholic Church, with its teachings and outward distinctives, is present from the very beginning. This stunning realization is what caused the nineteenth-century Anglican Protestant academic John Henry Newman to declare:

And this one thing at least is certain; whatever history teaches, whatever it omits, whatever it exaggerates or extenuates, whatever it says and unsays, at least the Christianity of history is not Protestantism. If ever there were a safe truth, it is this. And Protestantism has ever felt it so. I do not mean that every writer on the Protestant side has felt it; for it was the fashion at first, at least as a rhetorical argument against Rome, to appeal to past ages, or to some of them; but Protestantism, as a whole, feels it, and has felt it. This is shown in the determination already referred to of dispensing with historical Christianity altogether, and of forming a Christianity from the Bible alone: men never would have put it aside, unless they had despaired of it. . . . *To be deep in history is to cease to be a Protestant.*[7]

I discovered the Catholic Church was present in every century, every generation, from the present day all the way back to the apostles. The popes, the bishops, and those peculiarly Catholic doctrines, such as the Eucharist, can be seen in an unbroken line tracing all the way back to Christ.[8] As you go *back* in time, though, all the other Christian groups extant today begin to disappear. Century by century, toward the time of Christ, the Catholic Church is there—usually in its seemingly perpetual state of internal difficulties and external challenges, but there it is. All the other Christian groups that sprang up along the way vanish as you roll back the calendar. In the first century, what you *don't* find is "nondenominational" Christianity, no Calvinists, no Baptists, no Jehovah's Witnesses, no Mormons.

Christie's dad's proof-text arguments against Catholic traditions missed the ultimate biblical foundation behind them. The Catholic Church required time and reflection in order to develop its own theological vocabulary, a nomenclature of precise terminology with which it could adequately articulate its teachings to a world that often misunderstood or mischaracterized them. Terms such as "Trinity," "Incarnation," and "transubstantiation" are the result of this long and at times difficult process of forging a new vocabulary. Like the acorn and the oak tree, the Catholic Church in its infancy could not be expected to resemble the more mature Church of the present age. The Catholic Church is a divinely constituted living organism composed of human members, with Christ as the head of the body. For example, you won't find in the Acts of the Apostles any mention of titles such as "monsignor" or "archbishop" or a reference to "Vatican City." But this is to be expected, because the Catholic Church glimpsed in the pages of Acts is the infant Church, and it looked different from how it does now. The Catholic Church is just like the mustard seed Christ spoke about that grew from a tiny speck into a nearly tree-sized plant with many branches spreading out a great distance.

I am not suggesting that theological propositions—for example, the existence of God or the Real Presence of Christ in the Eucharist—are like atoms, azimuths, and animals, capable of being proved using science or mathematics. While there are objective, empirical methods for measuring, verifying, and even *dis*proving theological claims, they cannot be positively proved with mathematical certitude the way, for example, it can be proved that the area of a circle is equal to pi times its radius squared. The truth of Catholic teaching lies in the Church's biblical foundations and rich history, not in evidence gathered solely by the scientific method.

Truth is not always provable scientifically. The truth of love, for example, cannot be demonstrated on a chalkboard. We see and sense the effects of love, as well as the actions that so often betoken it (a kiss, a smile, a hug), but these are not "proof" that love is there. Judas, after all, betrayed Jesus with a kiss (see Matt. 26:47–50). We all know from experience that certain things are true, even if we cannot *prove* them scientifically. The love between husband and wife, parents' love for their children, etc. We have all the proof necessary to know these truths. Some are explicit (saying "I love you"), some are implicit (the father working long, tedious hours to support his family, or the mother who stays up all night tending to a sick child). Just so, the truth of the Catholic Church and its teachings can be borne out in explicit as well as implicit ways, the evidence itself as well as the logical, necessary conclusions and inferences that must follow from that evidence.

# 3

# Brought to My Senses

## THE SEVEN SACRAMENTS

THE SEVEN SACRAMENTS OF THE CATHOLIC CHURCH are the primary means by which God spiritually feeds, heals, and strengthens us. This is not to suggest that the sacraments are the *only* way God does things—far from it. He imparts grace however He wishes. But as the Bible shows, Christ gave the apostles certain specific ways of unleashing the power of God's grace known today as the sacraments. There are seven: baptism, confirmation, the Eucharist, confession, holy matrimony, holy orders, and holy anointing (aka extreme unction, the last rites).

Because God loves us and created us for happiness and freedom, through the sacraments He provides the remedies to heal and repair our self-inflicted wounds of sin. You can say that He is the Divine Physician. He's got the cure for what ails you. The cure is found in the sacraments of the Church, which accomplish several necessary things in the soul: animating the previously spiritually "inert" soul with sanctifying grace and, simultaneously, eradicating all sin[1] and its effects (baptism); healing our self-inflicted wounds of sin (confession and anointing of the sick); feeding the soul with the food of grace (the Holy Eucharist);[2] strengthening the soul for spiritual combat (confirmation, confession, holy anointing); and endowing the soul with the necessary power and capacity to carry out a particular calling (holy orders, holy matrimony). Each sacrament has its own function and purpose, though it is not mutually exclusive of the others or completely distinct from them in its grace-filled effects on the soul.

For example, one receives the Holy Spirit for the first time in the sacrament of baptism and, in a complementary way that is similar yet distinct, one experiences a new dimension of the indwelling presence of the Holy Spirit in the sacrament of confirmation. This is not to suggest that the Holy Spirit does not *fully* become present in the soul at baptism but rather that new and different gifts are imparted by him in confirmation. Similarly, in John 20:22, Jesus says to the apostles, "Receive the Holy Spirit," as he grants them the sacramental power to forgive sins. And then, several days later, the Holy Spirit comes down again on these same apostles in a new and complementary way on the Day of Pentecost (see Acts 2:4).

Each sacrament, in its own way, both strengthens and heals the soul, and some sacraments, such as baptism, confirmation, and holy orders, prepare and enable the soul for the reception of other sacraments and for particular forms of service to others. Consider the following helpful (though imperfect) analogy: We all know that mastering certain academic disciplines is a necessary prerequisite for mastering others. Take mathematics, for example. You must learn mathematics well and properly if you want to be an engineer. You would be obviously incapable of being a competent engineer if you did not understand and know how to use mathematics. But notice that before you can grasp the principles of and become proficient in mathematics, you must first master arithmetic—addition, subtraction, multiplication, and division. Imagine trying to learn algebra or trigonometry without the foundation of arithmetic! It would be impossible. It's the same way with the sacraments. Baptism is the foundational sacrament upon which all the others are grounded. It disposes, prepares, and enables the soul to receive the other sacraments. Without baptism, it would be impossible to validly receive the others.

Here's another way to think of it: Imagine you are a hundred miles from the ocean. You can't jump in and swim from there, no matter how much you might want to. But a car can *bring you* right to the shore so you *can* jump in.[3] Just as the car is necessary to the would-be swimmer, so is baptism necessary to the Christian, to enable him or her to "swim" in the limitless ocean of God's grace that comes to us, in this life, primarily through the sacraments.

Why doesn't God simply convey grace to us immediately, without the use of physical things like water, bread, and wine? Why doesn't He just "zap" us spiritually and be done with it? The answer to these reasonable questions lies in the fact that because God created human beings as composites of body and spirit, He cares for us bodily and spiritually through the medium of our senses. God *loves* matter—He created it, after all, and intends for us to benefit spiritually through material things. We all know this to be true, even if we don't give it much serious consideration. For example, you already know that eating some of your favorite comfort food can cheer you up when you're feeling sad or lonely. Food, which is material, has a real effect on your mood, emotions, and mental well-being, all of which are immaterial, or spiritual. (Just be careful how much comfort food you indulge in because, unlike the sacraments, it may cheer you up for a time but in the end will literally weigh you down.) The sacraments are composed of tangible elements like water and bread, but because Christ is working in them, they are vastly more than just symbols or metaphors for getting clean, satisfying hunger, and becoming strong and healthy. They actually *do* what they symbolize. You might say they are both symbols and the very realities they symbolize.

Many American Catholics over the age of fifty-five will remember learning about the sacraments (and indeed the rest of Catholic teaching) from the venerable *Baltimore Catechism,* which defined a sacrament as "an outward sign instituted by Christ that gives grace." There is a great deal of information packed into that small statement. Each of the seven sacraments is an outward sign, pointing to something beyond itself, but it is more than a mere sign the way a wedding ring is a sign that someone is married or the way a cane and dark glasses are signs that someone is physically blind. These signs, the sacraments, actually *do* what they signify. The Church identifies this set of seven sacred actions as having—intrinsic to each one—the power to convey sanctifying grace (i.e., the life of God). Each of these is an outward sign of an inward, unseen reality, and each is worked by Jesus Christ in the soul of the Christian who receives them.

The sacraments contain certain "matter" and "form" without which they are not true sacraments. They are *tangible* things that point to intangible, unseen realities. The water of baptism points to the cleansing of the soul; the Eucharistic bread and wine point toward the inward reality of feeding on the Bread of Life; the sacred chrism imposed on the forehead of the one being confirmed points to the inward strengthening of the soul as it takes its place as a "soldier of Christ."[4] The matter is the "stuff" of the sacrament—bread, wine, oil, chrism, water, and so forth—and the form is the correct words spoken when the sacrament is administered. For example, if someone were to attempt baptism with words other than those Christ himself gave—"in the name of the Father, and of the Son, and of the Holy Spirit" (Matt. 28:19)—it would not be a valid baptism. Likewise, if a priest did not say the words "I absolve you from your sins, in the name of the Father, and of the Son, and of the Holy Spirit," the sacrament of confession would not be valid.

Just as our bodies need nourishment to flourish, so, too, do our souls. The sacraments are to the soul what food, water, and medicine are to the body. In fact, there are many fascinating parallels between them. Without the soul, its "life principle," the body dies. And a disembodied soul, while eternal, nonetheless "limps" in some fashion because the soul is created by God to be united with the body.

The nature of the soul is to be a substance: a self-subsistent being. Because the soul is able to perform the actions of knowing and loving (corresponding to the intellect and the will) without the body, it therefore has the capacity to exist apart from the body. God has given each of us this rational ability, so we each have a duty to live out that ability to the fullest extent we are able. And this is how the sacraments help us. They not only convey grace to the souls through the medium of material things, they also convey a deeper understanding of *God Himself* through our senses. Just as the soul needs the senses to learn about the world, it needs the senses to learn about God.

Saint Paul says that the invisible things of God are clearly seen and are understood by the created things we encounter all around us (Rom. 1:20). God loves matter and is pleased to use physical things (bread, water, wine, oil) to convey grace—that way we may understand the unseen things by means of things we do see.

The *Catechism of the Catholic Church* uses a striking analogy to explain what happens when one receives a sacrament worthily: "As fire transforms into itself everything it touches, so the Holy Spirit transforms into the divine life whatever is subjected to his power."[5]

Three key effects are accomplished in the soul of one who receives the sacraments. First, the soul is further purified, cleansed from those base things that pose a barrier to God's holiness. Second, the soul is strengthened and inured against the corrosive effects of sin. And third, the soul's capacity for grace—in a sense, similar to the lungs' capacity to breathe in air—is expanded.

This is the meaning of the Church's affirmation that the sacraments act *ex opere operato* (Latin: from the work worked; literally, "by the very fact of the action's being performed");[6] that is, by virtue of the saving work of Christ, accomplished once for all. It follows that "the sacrament is not wrought by the righteousness of either the celebrant or the recipient, but by the power of God."[7] From the moment that a sacrament is celebrated in accordance with the intention of the Church, the power of Christ and his spirit acts in and through it, independent of the personal holiness of the minister. Nevertheless, the fruits of the sacraments also depend on the disposition of the one who receives them.

While it is easy to generalize and assume that "spirit is good" and "matter is bad," this flows from a misunderstanding of Christ's words that "the spirit is willing but the flesh is weak." The misunderstanding is that our weak flesh, which is wholly material, is somehow in itself bad and, therefore, it is wrongly assumed that God would not "dirty" Himself by using material things to convey grace. Such suspicion of matter still hampers many people's willingness to accept the sacraments. But certain biblical truths can help to ameliorate and, hopefully, eliminate such negative attitudes. These include the creation account in Genesis, where it says repeatedly that "God saw that it was good" each time He brought some new element of the cosmos into existence. And upon creating human beings (with souls *and* bodies, keep in mind), Scripture tells us that God said this was "very good."

God loves matter. If He didn't, and if matter were not in

itself good, He would not have created it. In fact, if matter were not good He *could* not have created it, for to have done so would be contrary to His nature as an all-good God. He cannot be the author of anything evil, because that would go against His nature. This is not to say that, after the fact, material things cannot become corrupted (cancer, smog, and our own sinful human natures after the fall of Adam and Eve are sufficient proof that they can be debased). Rather, because matter itself is essentially good and because human beings are creatures composed of matter and spirit, it makes perfect sense that the Lord would institute sacraments to advance the health and well-being of all who receive them worthily.

These great gifts of grace that the sacraments impart are so important and so majestic because we are all so utterly *unworthy*. As Saint Paul says, "God shows his love for us in that while we were yet sinners Christ died for us" (Rom. 5:8). And the beautiful part about it is that, even though we yet remain sinners, Christ's grace is poured into our hearts through the sacraments to help save us from our sins. The Catholic writer Mark Shea explains it this way:

> Once you've faced the fact that humans are sinners, you are halfway to understanding the real essence and purpose of the Catholic Church: to satisfy our need of salvation in Christ. Baptism is not a magic spell that makes you a Shiny Happy Person. It is the first install-ment of a lifelong program of chemotherapy against an aggressive and deadly form of cancer in the soul and in our culture. Catholics are a people on the road

to recovery. Not a people who do not face setbacks. But without the treatment we don't escape the cancer. We just die faster.[8]

Catholics speak about "grace" in a few specific ways—in particular, "actual grace" and "sanctifying grace." Actual grace is external to the soul. It is a prompting of the Holy Spirit that nudges us to head in the right direction. You might think of actual grace like a tugboat whose job is to nudge an ocean liner out of its dock and toward the open sea. Sanctifying grace is internal to the soul; it's inside you and "inheres" in the soul in a way analogous to how blood is inside the body and inheres in every part of it, vivifying all the members down to the smallest cell. Sanctifying grace is the life of the Blessed Trinity poured into the soul. When we receive sanctifying grace through the sacraments, God literally fills us with His own life, expanding our capacity for Him. This is why holy people seem to progress in holiness. The more you get, the greater your capacity becomes to receive more. Conversely, those who willfully reject and turn away from God's grace become spiritually stunted, withered, and atrophied. In their case, what little virtue they may have had gradually ebbs away, and their capacity to be filled with God's love and grace also diminishes.

I like to think of the Catholic Church as being in the "solutions business." It is a two-thousand-year-old global organization with a proven track record of success that is dedicated to providing the solutions to life's most urgent problems, dilemmas, and challenges. Its CEO, Jesus Christ, knows exactly what human beings need to live healthy, happy, fulfilling lives based on truth, goodness, and love—everything everyone wants, even if not everyone is consciously aware of these things. And he has put in place exactly the right delivery system to ensure that these solutions his Church offers the world can be obtained simply, easily, and at no cost. The most fundamental of these are the sacraments. They are not the sole set of solutions, but they form the foundation upon which other solutions, such as the Holy Bible, Apostolic Tradition, prayer, service to others, the arts, science, and everything else can be built. To understand better how the sacraments act as the primary, foundational set of his solutions, let's consider what the sacraments are and what they do, beginning with the definition of the term.

The word "sacrament" has its etymological roots in the Latin word *sacramentum,* which means a "holy thing," as well as a sacred "oath," the kind by which, for example, Roman soldiers would swear their loyalty to the emperor upon being inducted into the army.[9] Very early on the Catholic Church adopted *sacramentum* and its Greek cognate *mysterion.* This is why, traditionally, the sacraments have also been known as the "holy mysteries." As the *Catechism of the Catholic Church* explains:

> The Greek word *mysterion* was translated into Latin by two terms: *mysterium* and *sacramentum.* In later usage the term *sacramentum* emphasizes the visible sign of the hidden reality of salvation which was indicated by the term *mysterium.* In this sense, Christ himself is the mys-

tery of salvation: "For there is no other mystery of God, except Christ."[10] The saving work of his holy and sanctifying humanity is the sacrament of salvation, which is revealed and active in the Church's sacraments (which the Eastern Churches also call "the holy mysteries"). The seven sacraments are the signs and instruments by which the Holy Spirit spreads the grace of Christ the head throughout the Church which is his Body. The Church, then, both contains and communicates the invisible grace she signifies. It is in this analogical sense that the Church is called a "sacrament."[11]

Not only did Christ personally institute the seven sacraments,[12] it is his power working in the sacraments that makes them efficacious. It is not from the priest or even the Church itself that the sacraments derive their awesome, life-changing spiritual power; it is solely from Christ because it is he who is present and working in each of the sacraments, through the ministry of the Church. This is analogous to the nuclear energy contained within the reactor of a nuclear submarine. When that power is present, the submarine can do what submarines are designed and built to do: move freely throughout the ocean. But if that nuclear power is absent, the sub can do nothing. It simply cannot achieve its "submarineness." In the same way, Christ's presence and power in the sacraments enable them to do what they symbolize and, as a result, they enable human beings to fully achieve their humanness.

The sacraments accomplish three essential things for us: (1) They initiate us into an intimate relationship with

God that, while incomplete and imperfect in this life (due to *our* imperfections and lack of wholeness), will transform us into the perfect, whole, and complete beings God wants us to be in the eternal life to come; (2) they heal us from our self-inflicted wounds of sin and weakness; and (3) they empower and enable us to go forward in life and fulfill our individual, personalized callings that God invites us to embrace and live out. Let's consider them in that order.

## Initiation

The next time you step onto an airplane for a cross-country trip, glance to your left at the pilots sitting in the cockpit performing their preflight checks. No doubt you've already done this often enough and, chances are, you've never given it a second thought. I mean, you've never stopped and *wondered* if the pilots actually knew how to fly the plane, right? That's because you already have good, demonstrable grounds to be certain that they do. How? Well, for one, their uniforms designate them as being pilots. This is an *outward sign of the inward reality* of their aeronautical expertise. Also, they are in the cockpit doing what pilots do to prepare for a flight. Airlines don't allow anyone in there who is not trained and duly authorized to be there. All of this explicit evidence points to an explicit truth that you and I take for granted as true each time we step aboard a jetliner: the pilots have been *initiated* into the science of flying airplanes. They have been systematically introduced to this science and thoroughly trained in its fine details. Without this initiation—flight school, lectures, books, exams, simulator training, and so forth—they would be incapable of actually piloting a plane. The same is true of any important profession. For example, it takes years for physicians and engineers to be initiated into their highly technical, complex fields of practice. Without the necessary preparation (i.e., initiation), pilots, physicians, and engineers could not fulfill their appointed duties.

In a similar way, the sacraments of baptism, confirmation, and the Holy Eucharist initiate the believer into the fullness of the holy mysteries of God's grace by not only introducing him or her to the supernatural life of God's grace but also preparing him or her to receive the other sacraments and benefit to the fullest extent from the special graces they impart.

As a result of the fall into sin of our First Parents, Adam and Eve, the whole human race, each one of us, suffers the consequences of being conceived in the state of original sin. Original sin is not an essence or a reality, the way a stain or a scar is; rather, it is a condition of lacking a due good (i.e., a necessary good), the absence of something necessary that *should* be there but isn't. Imagine a wingless bird, a blind painter, a singer with no vocal cords. The due good missing in us is grace, God's own life. Think of how a vast fortune could be lost to the children if the father and mother squandered it or forfeited it by committing a crime. This is how our grace was lost through Adam and Eve's original sin.

Because they were swindled by the lying Serpent, the rest of humanity is born into a state of spiritual bankruptcy, as paupers who have been preemptively defrauded of that vast inheritance God had originally intended for us to possess. Baptism initiates us back into that world of being rightful heirs, adopted sons and daughters of the Lord, who have a legitimate claim on all He has promised to those who love and obey Him. Without the spiritual reinstatement that baptism provides, we would remain perpetually penniless in a spiritual sense, forever on the outside looking in.

Known in the Eastern Churches as "chrismation,"[13] the sacrament of confirmation is a further initiation into the life of God's grace. It's a coming-of-age that enables us to actually begin making full use of the inheritance bequeathed to us from the Living God but which we are, as yet, not mature enough to handle with full responsibility and resourcefulness. Through the sacrament of confirmation, Christians are "more perfectly bound to the Church and are enriched with a special strength of the Holy Spirit. Hence they are, as true witnesses of Christ, more strictly obliged to spread and defend the faith by word and deed."[14] This does not mean that confirmation is only for those chronologically old enough to explain and defend the faith. In an older form of the sacrament of confirmation, the bishop gave a small tap to the cheek of the young person being confirmed. It was a symbol of his or her new role of being a "soldier for Christ," which might bring opposition and even persecution.[15]

## Healing

When you get a paper cut or accidentally prick your finger with a pin, you instinctively put it in your mouth, don't you? We all do. Why? Because our saliva contains certain enzymes that kill bacteria and promote healing. This powerful, innate human instinct to heal wounds isn't just a matter of common sense. It derives from our unspoken realization that an untreated wound, especially one that is serious, will likely worsen and lead to sickness, suffering, and even death. Well, the human soul is no different from the body in this regard. It, too, requires healing when wounded by sin.

When, through sin, we get "bitten" by the ancient Serpent, the sacraments heal us by "sucking out the poison" of death, cleaning the wound, binding it, and applying the healing balm of God's grace to restore us to spiritual health and vitality. Do not underestimate the sacraments' tremendous power to heal! We are all sick with the malaria of sin—some of us more desperately than others—contracted not from the bite of a mosquito but from the bite of an apple.[16]

The deadly pathogen of sin exploits our weaknesses when attacking us. We are weakened in the face of temptations because of original sin, in particular from a devastating effect of original sin known as "concupiscence," a term that comes from the Latin term *concupiscentia,* meaning "cupidity," a strong, even violent desire for something or someone. It's part of the raw human condition that, because of original sin, we all must contend with, each in our own way: a will that is weak and quite susceptible slip-sliding away down that slippery slope of our disordered inclination toward sin. Through the strength He provides in the sacraments God offers us a way to avoid that danger.

Let's face it. We all struggle with temptations to sin. You do. I do. We experience intense longings for something, or even many things, such as sexual pleasure, or material possessions, or the comfortably numb buzz that alcohol induces, or drugs, or revenge, or power, or honors and human respect. The list is a long one, and most of us have to contend with not just one or two objects of our cupidity but with many, some much more attractive than others.

The sacraments, especially baptism, confession, and the Holy Eucharist, are powerful antidotes to combat and suppress our concupiscence in a way reminiscent of how certain drugs, such as quinine and chloroquine, suppress the parasite that causes malaria. It just makes sense that if you have the antidote to what ails you—which is exactly what the sacraments are, powerful grace-filled remedies of God's love for us—you take it! One would wonder about the sanity of a person suffering from a serious, indeed fatal, condition who refuses to take a doctor's prescription for the medicine that can cure him.

Catholic moral theologian Mark Lowery uses the analogy of an orchestra conductor to explain how and why Christ heals us through the sacraments, especially confession (reconciliation):

We only enjoy a piece of music when it is properly ordered—everything in tune, everyone playing the right notes, just the right way, together. When something is out of order (there is a lack of "due order"), we appreciate the person who fixes it—the conductor—with a call for more careful tuning, for more accurate rhythm, or for one instrument to be quieter and another louder.

No one is interested in *placing blame* on anyone—that's a separate issue. Rather, proper order is needed so that the audience, and the musicians themselves, can be truly happy. So the conductor who fixes the problem must not be afraid to be very direct about what constitutes lack of due order, and very direct about how to fix it. Again, the conductor isn't first interested in *blaming* (assigning culpability to) one musician or another, but in keeping the whole symphony on track.

In a similar way, when Christ says, "I forgive you" (sacramentally, through the priest), those are the happiest words imaginable and they could not be spoken unless the individual had first been pointed in the right direction. Sin . . . is what constitutes the wrong direction, or lack of due order. That is why sin is called . . . a *privation*. It prevents us from being aligned with true happiness.[17]

## Service

The sacraments also equip us to serve others. They do this by first softening up our hearts with God's grace so that we will, more and more, see Jesus in others and seek to help them for the love of Jesus. In Matthew 25:31–46, Jesus tells us that at the end of the world he will come again to judge the nations. The righteous, whose destiny is eternal life, he describes as sheep, and the damned as goats. It's a familiar teaching, though its deeper meaning can be obscured by that familiarity: Those who feed the hungry, give drink to the thirsty, welcome the stranger, clothe the naked, and visit the sick and imprisoned, he says, will be saved. Those who deliberately fail to do these things will be damned. Why? Because, as Jesus says, "Truly, I say to you, as you did it [or failed to do it] to one of the least of these my brethren, you did it [or failed to do it] to me."

Now, without question, there are countless sincere and generous people who are not Catholic, who do not receive the sacraments, and who yet *do* many good deeds of service for others. This is praiseworthy, of course. But the power of God's grace in the sacraments can take those natural acts of human kindness and transform them into supernatural acts of great spiritual value. They are, as Saint Paul says in Romans 1:5, the good fruit borne by the "obedience of faith."[18]

The second way the sacraments equip us to serve others is by their power to endow the soul of the one receiving the sacrament with certain capacities previously absent. In the case of holy orders, these include the ability to forgive sins (John 20:21–23; 2 Cor. 5:18–21), to offer the Eucharistic Sacrifice, and to ordain other men to the priesthood.[19] This priestly, sacramental service in the Church of the New Covenant is the perfected completion of something remarkable and often overlooked that happened to the Israelites during the time of Moses.[20] All members of the Twelve

Tribes of Israel were called "priests" and regarded themselves as such, inasmuch as all understood they were expected to offer a sacrifice of praise to God through prayer and upright, righteous living. God had blessed them as a people "set apart" from the Gentiles, further underscoring the holiness to which He was calling them: "You shall be to me a kingdom of priests and a holy nation" (Exod. 19:6). But God then established one of the tribes, Levi, to be set apart as a caste of priests who would minister to the entire kingdom of priests (see Num. 1:48–53; Josh. 13:33).

These Old Testament priests served the people in various ways—most important, by offering sacrifices on their behalf, beseeching God to forgive His people and make them holy.

The New Testament priesthood established by Christ at the Last Supper is a subordinate share in his own high priesthood (see Heb. 4:14–16, 5:1–10).

Deacons, priests, and bishops are ordained to serve. As spiritual fathers, priests and bishops fulfill many roles of service that directly parallel the service performed by earthly fathers, such as giving us life through the regenerating waters of baptism, healing our wounds of sin through confession and holy anointing, and feeding us with the Bread of Life in the Holy Eucharist.

This is why Saint Paul reminds us that, "though you have countless guides in Christ, you do not have many fathers. *For I became your father in Christ Jesus through the gospel.* I urge you, then, be imitators of me" (1 Cor. 4:15–16).[21]

# 4

## Soul Food

### MASS AND THE HOLY EUCHARIST

EVERY SUCCESSFUL GLOBAL BRAND HAS AN INSTANTLY identifiable logo that sets it apart from the crowd. Think of McDonald's golden arches, Amazon's smiling box, Apple's apple.

And though the Catholic Church isn't a "brand" and doesn't have an official logo,[1] a key reason it's been so universally recognizable for two thousand years is the Mass, during which the sacrament of the Eucharist is "confected." Catholics call this the miracle of transubstantiation, in which the substance (i.e., reality) of bread and wine are replaced by the power of God's grace with the substance of the Risen Christ, body, blood, soul, and divinity.

Even those who know little about the Catholic Church know that Catholics "go to Mass."

The English word "Mass" derives from the Latin term *missio,* meaning "mission," "sending," or "dismissal." In the traditional Latin form of the Mass, the final words spoken by the priest at the conclusion are *"Ite, missa est,"* which roughly translates as "Go, you are dismissed." Early on, when the Latin term *missio* had become synonymous with the Eucharistic Sacrifice itself, the liturgical meaning of this phrase became fixed as "Go, the Mass is finished."[2]

Jesus celebrated the very first Mass at the Last Supper, not long after sundown on Holy Thursday, A.D. 33, when "he took bread, and when he had given thanks [Greek: *Eucharistein*], he broke it and gave it to them, saying, 'This is my body which is given for you. Do this in remembrance of me.' And likewise the chalice after supper, saying, 'This chalice which is poured out for you is the new covenant in my blood.'[3] With these startling words, Christ inaugurated a new reality for the fledgling Church he was establishing, one in which he would remain truly and substantially present in the Church, until the end of time, when he will return to judge the nations. This was the faith of the earliest Christians, as testified to by leading figures of the young Church, such as Saint Ignatius of Antioch, who would be martyred around 107. He was a disciple of John the apostle and learned the doctrine of the Eucharist directly from him, an *eyewitness* to the Last Supper. "Take note," he said, "of those who hold heterodox opinions on the grace of Jesus Christ which has come to us, and see how contrary their opinions are to the mind of God. . . . They abstain from the Eucharist and from prayer because they do not confess that the Eucharist is the flesh of our Savior Jesus Christ, flesh which suffered for our sins and which that Father, in his goodness, raised up again. They who deny the gift of God are perishing in their disputes."[4]

These early Catholics, some of whom, like Ignatius of Antioch, knew the apostles personally, were adamant that the Eucharist they celebrated was not merely a symbol of Jesus, nor was it only a memorial meal. Rather, they insisted, they had received from the apostles themselves the teaching that when Christ said "this is my body" and "this is my blood" he meant it literally. Ignatius wrote: "I have no taste for corruptible food nor for the pleasures of this life. I desire the bread of God, which is the flesh of Jesus Christ, who was of the seed of David; and for drink I desire his blood, which is love incorruptible" (*Epistle to the Romans* 7:3). This is no macabre fascination but, rather, a stalwart early Christian testimony to the reality that Christ placed the Eucharist at the very center of the Christian life.

Many important Church Fathers, such as Justin Martyr (100–165),[5] Irenaeus of Lyons (130–202),[6] and Clement of Alexandria (150–215),[7] provide a wealth of clear and emphatic statements about the centrality of the Mass and the Real Presence of Christ in the Eucharist, repeatedly stating that this teaching had been delivered to the Church directly by the apostles. For example, Saint Irenaeus wrote:

> If the Lord were from other than the Father, how could he rightly take bread, which is of the same creation as our own, and confess it to be his body and affirm that the mixture in the cup is his blood? . . . He has declared the cup, a part of creation, to be his own blood, from which he causes our blood to flow; and the bread, a part of creation, he has established as his own body, from which he gives increase unto our bodies. When,

therefore, the mixed cup [wine and water] and the baked bread receives the Word of God and becomes the Eucharist, the body of Christ, and from these the substance of our flesh is increased and supported, how can they say that the flesh is not capable of receiving the gift of God, which is eternal life—flesh which is nourished by the body and blood of the Lord, and is in fact a member of him? (*Against Heresies,* 4:33–32; 5:2)

It's worth noting that at the end of the first century, when Ignatius of Antioch and others wrote about the Eucharist, the Catholic Church did not yet possess the precise theological vocabulary it would eventually develop over time and after tremendous prayerful, biblical, and theological reflection and study. And this stands to reason, of course. The Church was still under a more or less constant pressure from bloody persecution, primarily at the hands of the Roman Empire. So its leading theologians, Scripture scholars, and apologists did not have the luxury of unimpeded opportunities and plenty of time to write more on this and other important doctrinal subjects. When they did write about this issue, it was with a vigor and clarity that is impressive in its unswerving commitment to the apostolic teaching that, at the Last Supper, Jesus Christ instituted the Mass and the Eucharist, the former a liturgical action that brings the latter into existence, for the spiritual health, well-being, and building up of God's people.

Over a thousand years later, the Catholic Church adopted the technical term "transubstantiation"[8] to better explain what happens to the bread and wine at Mass. As the word suggests, the substance (i.e., reality) of the bread and wine is replaced by the substance of the glorified, Risen Christ, who becomes really and truly present *under the appearances* of bread and wine.

The appearances of a thing are not the thing itself. For example, picture in your mind a red, rubber, bouncy ball.[9] The color red of the ball is not the ball itself, nor is the texture, the bounciness, or even its round shape. Each of these distinguishing characteristics, indeed any distinguishing characteristic that our senses can detect, is an "accident," or a property, of that red, rubber, bouncy ball, but none of them is the ball itself. This is a powerful truth! And what it means, as far as the Mass is concerned, is that, at the consecration, what was previously bread and wine ceases to be bread and wine and becomes the Risen, glorified Body, Blood, Soul, and Divinity of Christ even though the texture, color, taste, and molecular structure of bread and wine remain.

In other words, this miracle is undetectable by human senses. What was bread before the consecration continues to taste and feel like bread. If one were to consume enough of the Precious Blood, one would become inebriated because the properties of wine, including its alcoholic content, remain.[10] The doctrine of transubstantiation was not "invented" in 1215, any more than the doctrine of the Trinity was "invented" in 325 when the First Council of Nicaea formally defined it—One God in Three Persons. In each case, the Church had to specifically and officially enunciate precisely what it teaches so as to avoid any ambiguity and thus wiggle room for heretical notions.[11] Saint Justin Martyr underscored the need for certainty on this teaching:

> We call this food Eucharist, and no one else is permitted to partake of it, except one who believes our teaching to be true and who has been washed in the washing which is for the remission of sins and for regeneration and is thereby living as Christ enjoined. For not as common bread nor common drink do we receive these; but since Jesus Christ our Savior was made incarnate by the word of God and had both flesh and blood for our salvation, so too, as we have been taught, the food which has been made into the Eucharist by the Eucharistic prayer set down by him, and by the change of which our blood and flesh is nurtured, is both the flesh and the blood of that incarnated Jesus. (*First Apology*, chap. 66)

Because the Mass is so central to the Catholic Church, the way the heart is central to the body, it's no surprise that Catholic theologians going all the way back to apostolic times were exceedingly careful to defend and proclaim the Mass as a sacrifice and the Eucharist as the participation in the very Body and Blood of the Lord that he sacrificed for us on the cross.

The Mass really is the once-for-all sacrifice of Christ on the cross *re-presented* to us here and now, in time and space. It's a truly mind-blowing concept, one that for twenty centuries now has and continues to inspire countless men and women around the world to leave everything behind and become Catholic. They are like the man who sells everything to obtain the "pearl of great value," about which Jesus spoke (see Matt. 13:45–46).[12] At Mass, we are made truly present at the Last Supper, at Calvary, and in the heavenly sanctuary, in which Christ our High Priest eternally offers himself to the Father for our redemption and salvation. No matter how majestic or dreary the setting, or how inspiring or bland the priest, the profound spiritual reality of the Mass is beyond the power of our senses to apprehend. In Hebrews 7:24 Jesus's priesthood is described in the Greek as *aparabatos,* meaning permanent, unchanging, eternal. It cannot pass away or become obsolete.

The primary function of the priesthood is to offer sacrifice. This is true of the Old Testament priests, whose imperfect, symbolical, and provisional ministry was established by God through Moses. It is true most fully of Jesus himself, as he offered the perfect sacrifice for sins by giving his own life for ours. And it is true of Catholic priests, who offer the Holy Sacrifice of the Mass on altars around the world, every minute of every day. This fact, by the way, fulfills biblical prophecy, which states: "For from the rising of the sun to its setting my name is great among the nations, and in every place incense is offered to my name, and a pure offering; for my name is great among the nations, says the LORD of hosts" (Mal. 1:11).

The Mass is dependent upon there being validly ordained priests who can celebrate it. No priests = no Mass. No Mass = no Eucharist. And, no Eucharist would effectively = no Church. At the Last Supper, Christ the High

Priest instituted the sacrament of holy orders by initiating his apostles into the priestly identity they would live out until martyrdom claimed them. When he commanded them to "do this in memory of me," he simultaneously empowered them with his grace to actually *do* what he told them to do.

Christ himself is our High Priest: "For it was fitting that we should have such a high priest, holy, blameless, unstained, separated from sinners, exalted above the heavens. He has no need, like those high priests [i.e., the priests of the Old Covenant inaugurated by Moses], to offer sacrifices daily, first for his own sins and then for those of the people; he did this once for all when he offered up himself" (Heb. 7:26–27). Those Old Covenant sacrifices actually accomplished nothing in themselves. They could only symbolize and point toward the true, permanent, and perfect sacrifice of Christ. Those former sacrifices, endlessly taking place in the temple, did not take away sin. But the sacrifice of Christ on the cross did and does. And at each Mass, Catholics receive from Christ the High Priest the spiritual benefits he won for us on the cross. This reality transcends time and space and yet encompasses each person present at Mass in time and space.

The Mass is to the Catholic Church what an engine is to a car, or what wings are to an eagle, or what musical instruments are to an orchestra. Without an engine, a car is a useless hulk, incapable of doing what cars are made for. Eagles must fly, or they'll die. The very thought of a wingless eagle is disturbing—a freak of nature, a living oxymoron. Imagine an orchestra, a large ensemble of trained musicians who have no instruments. They gather together, but for what purpose? No instruments = no music. And because an orchestra's sole purpose is to make music, what would be the point? Just so, the Catholic Church needs the Mass because, without it, her purpose and function and mission would not exist.

Jesus Christ could have arranged things in any number of different ways, including, perhaps, establishing his Church without the Mass and the Eucharist. But that would be the functional equivalent of forming an orchestra but not giving the musicians any musical instruments, and then instructing them to simply go around *talking about* music to audiences, *describing* what music sounds like rather than actually playing music. That would be an absurd situation. But Jesus's actions and teachings are the furthest things from absurd, as anyone who encounters him in the Four Gospels knows. He never does anything that is haphazard, halfway, or hollow. Rather, his actions are always enduring, effectual, and extraordinary.

And yet, many sincere people still fail to see and understand the biblical roots of the Eucharist and the Mass, mainly, I believe, because no one has ever explained it to them. I still remember one day when Christie and I were hanging out by her pool. Her dad had spent the last half hour trying to convince me that the Catholic teaching on the Real Presence of Christ in the Eucharist[13] is a diabolical false doctrine. He went into the house and returned a few moments later with a Chick tract,[14] which he handed me. Its title? "The Death Cookie." In an absurdly garish, comic book format, this little pamphlet (with a sinister skull and crossbones superimposed over a Communion host used at Mass) purported to demonstrate how the Catholic teaching on the Eucharist came about. Sometime during the Middle Ages (judging from the costumes), the devil convinced a nameless, debauched-looking con man that if he wanted to gain control over the people all he needed to do was pose as their religious "papa," or pope, and then inveigle them into believing that he had the power to make God come down into a "holy cookie," which is shown as a host. This "cookie god" motif was being borrowed wholesale, the devil tells him, from the ancient Egyptians.

"I love it!" the con man exclaims. "If *they* could do it, then so can we!"

"And so the Holy Work began," the tract informed me. "Papa and his Holy Helpers put on religious costumes and the people were dazzled." The tract then depicts these "Holy Helpers," who are dressed as Catholic monks, intoning *"hocus pocus domi nocus"*[15] over a cookie/host with the fingers of both hands extended toward it as if arcs of electricity would flow from them.

The tract is laughable in its lowbrow, ham-fisted misrepresentation of this Catholic teaching. And I told Christie's dad this to his face. In fact, I laughed out loud after reading the first page of the silly screed. That wasn't the reaction he was expecting. I guess I had become more confident and willing to stick up for my beliefs as the summer wore on. He challenged me to disprove what it said, and with that, I had a new mission in life. I dove into the Bible and the reference works in my parents' library, finding more and more evidence that refuted the claims made in the tract. I discovered the wide and deep testimony to the Real Presence of Christ in the Eucharist among the Early Church Fathers (some of whom, like Saint Ignatius of Antioch, knew the apostles *personally*). Their defense of the Catholic doctrine of the Eucharist utterly destroyed the claims made in "The Death Cookie," on historical grounds alone.

More important, though, I found that the New Testament is replete with biblical evidence teaching the importance and centrality of this doctrine.

In John 6:35, Jesus declares, "I am the bread of life; he who comes to me shall not hunger, and he who believes in me shall never thirst." This is part of the preamble of his "Bread of Life" discourse in which he reveals the doctrine of the Eucharist. He knows how powerful and pressing our human desire is for the truth, for meaning and fulfillment, for happiness. And he promises that all of these things will be granted in superabundance through the Eucharist. Our hunger and thirst for these things will not be satisfied and slaked merely by "believing" in him, if by that we assume that our faith alone can save us. No, Jesus's teaching here is that coming to him in faith is the means by which we become able to partake of his great gift of himself in the Eucharist.

"I am the living bread," he says, "which came down from heaven; if any one eats of this bread, he will live forever; and the bread which I shall give for the life of the world is my flesh. . . . Truly, truly, I say to you, unless you eat the flesh of the Son of man and drink his blood, you have no life in you; he who eats my flesh and drinks my blood has eternal life, and I will raise him up at the last day. For my flesh is food indeed, and my blood is drink indeed" (John 6:48; 51–55).

This was simply too outrageous for the crowd. They rumbled and grumbled and complained, "How can this man give us his flesh to *eat?*"

Jesus, though, seeing their agitation, not only did not back down, he upped the ante by pressing home the literal meaning of his teachings:

> Whoever eats my flesh and drinks my blood remains in me and I in him. Just as the living Father sent me and I have life because of the Father, so also the one who feeds on me will have life because of me.
>
> This is the bread that came down from heaven. Unlike your ancestors who ate and still died, whoever eats this bread will live forever. (John 6:56–58)

The Jews' consternation over this teaching on the Eucharist was palpable. Many simply could not abide it. "This is a hard saying," they scoffed. "Who can listen to it?" John's Gospel describes how many of Christ's erstwhile followers abandoned him at that point because they simply couldn't bring themselves to accept this outrageous claim. Note also what Jesus does and doesn't do in the wake of the crowd's repudiation of him and his teaching. He did not try to stop them. He didn't call out to those who were walking away in anger, saying, "Wait! You misunderstood me. I didn't mean all that stuff *literally,* I meant it figuratively. You know, like eating bread that symbolizes me." This notion (i.e., that Jesus was only speaking figuratively here) was what Christie's dad had been trying so hard to get me to accept.

Not only does Jesus not try to correct their understanding of his teaching, he turns to his apostles and says, "Will you also leave?" Simon Peter's response is the very one I found myself repeating each time I encountered biblical or historical arguments against the Catholic teaching on the Real Presence of Christ in the Eucharist. He said, "Lord, to whom shall we go? You have the words of eternal life." For me, as I grappled with all the various arguments against this Catholic teaching (indeed, on the sacraments in general), I found myself uttering the same words, "Lord, to whom shall I go? You have the words of eternal life and, wonderfully, I am able to receive you as the Bread of Life in the Catholic Church."

Every time I read this statement it reminds me of how being Catholic does not require that I fully comprehend every truth God proposes to me. I'm quite certain that Simon Peter's public profession of faith in Christ, and in his Eucharistic teaching, was accompanied by a significant sense of awe and wonder at this new doctrine that, while true because Christ proclaimed it, was mysterious and incredibly difficult to wrap one's mind around. Christ's "Will you also leave?" is not an expression of defeatism. No, it is a galvanizing invitation to faith. Because his teaching on the Eucharist—"my flesh is real food, my blood is real drink"—is so radical, he knows that some will fall away because it's just too hard a teaching to accept, but countless others will embrace this truth so wholeheartedly that many of them, such as Saint Ignatius of Antioch, willingly suffer the cruelties of martyrdom rather than deny this great truth.[16] As Saint Cyril of Jerusalem observed:

> The bread and the wine of the Eucharist before the holy invocation of the adorable Trinity were simple bread and wine, but the invocation having been made, the bread becomes the body of Christ and the wine the blood of Christ. . . . Do not, therefore, regard the bread and wine as simply that; for they are, according to the Master's declaration, the body and blood of Christ. Even though the senses suggest to you the other, let faith make you firm. Do not judge in this matter by taste, but be fully assured by the faith, not doubting that you have been deemed worthy of the body and blood of Christ. . . . [Being] fully convinced that the apparent bread is not bread, even though it is sensible to the taste, but the body of Christ, and that the apparent wine is not wine, even though the taste would have it so, . . . partake of that bread as something spiritual, and put a cheerful face on your soul. (*Catechetical Lectures,* 19:7; 22:6, 9)

There is no other option for me as a Catholic than to remain in the Church, because it is there that Christ is most fully present, in the tabernacle and on the altar, in the Blessed Sacrament of the Eucharist. I have participated in many informal debates on the Eucharist, including with

Protestant ministers, and in all my interactions with those who deny the Catholic doctrine of the Eucharist and heap up endless arguments against it, I always come away more firmly convinced that the Catholic teaching is true, despite the sincerity and good intentions of those who oppose it and their many arguments.

Many people have heard of the famed Eucharistic miracles of the Catholic Church; for example, when the bread and wine at Mass become human flesh and blood. One of the most amazing miracles happened in the eighth century in a small Italian village known today as Lanciano. We don't have to rely on pious folklore for the details. In fact, the miracle itself is still present today, even after having been exposed to the elements, handling by priests and bishops, sunlight, flash photography, and so forth. A Catholic priest who was experiencing serious doubts about the Catholic doctrine of the Real Presence of Christ in the Eucharist was celebrating Mass one morning when, as he pronounced the words of consecration (i.e., the words of Christ at the Last Supper, "This is my body which will be given up for you" and "This is the chalice of my blood . . . which shall be poured out for you and for many"), the bread and wine on the altar were miraculously transformed into living human flesh and blood. Both have been rigorously tested by the tools of modern science, but there is no scientific explanation for how they continue to exist intact after twelve centuries! The flesh is from living heart tissue, and the blood, which is type AB, contains all the elements present in normal, healthy, human blood.[17] To this day, believers and skeptics alike travel to Lanciano to see this Eucharistic miracle. Scientists have not been able to explain it, nor have atheists been able to debunk it. It's there for all to see.

Some years ago, I myself experienced what might be considered a kind of Eucharistic miracle. It was a sad story that (just barely) turned out to have a happy ending.

In the early 1990s, Father Isaiah Bennett, a priest in Brooklyn, New York, invited me to visit his parish to conduct a weekend apologetics seminar on Mormonism and the Jehovah's Witnesses, two groups whose aggressive proselytization in that neighborhood had steadily been siphoning off Catholics from his congregation. The weekend went well. Many people attended and the interest level was high. After the Saturday sessions were finished, Father Isaiah and I went to dinner, over which he told me of his own great interest in Catholic apologetics with Mormons. It would not be an exaggeration to say that his "interest" in Mormonism was actually something bordering on obsession. He told me that he read everything about Mormonism he could get his hands on out of a desire to know how best to discuss religion with Mormon missionaries and prevent his fellow Catholics from leaving the Church. The following day, I returned home to San Diego, where I was living at the time, and I really didn't think about that weekend's events or Father Isaiah much after that.

A few years passed. Then, one day, out of the blue, I got a call from Robert, a Mormon acquaintance of mine in Los Angeles. His voice was excited, almost gleeful.

"Patrick, you'll never guess who visited as the guest speaker at our stake center[18] this past Sunday! He said he knows you."

"Hmm," I said, "you're right. I'll never guess. Who was it?"

"*Isaiah Bennett!*" he said, sounding quite pleased.

"What?" I asked in confusion. "The only Isaiah Bennett I know is a Catholic priest out in New York. Why on earth would a Mormon congregation invite a Catholic priest to come speak?"

"That's just it. He's not a priest anymore. He's not a Catholic anymore. He converted to the Mormon Church two years ago! Now he's giving lectures at Mormon venues about why he left Catholicism to become Mormon."

My heart sank at this distressing and wholly unanticipated news.

"Isaiah told me he'd like you to call him," Robert added blithely and then gave me his number.

I realized what was happening. I'm sure Robert was thinking something along the lines of, well, we got Isaiah Bennett, and next we'll get Patrick Madrid. Then, we'll get Scott Hahn, and then Mother Angelica, and so forth. He practically begged me to be sure I called Isaiah as soon as possible.

I was so depressed. How could this possibly have happened? I wondered what I myself might have done to foment such a bizarre step on the part of Father Isaiah—the very priest at whose parish I had spent a weekend trying to inoculate Catholics against the lure of Mormonism! I felt like such a failure.

Not wanting to talk to anyone that day, I let all my calls go to voice mail. As I was leaving my office, the phone kept ringing, going to voice mail, then ringing again. Someone obviously wanted very badly to reach me, but I was in no mood to talk and went home.

The following morning, I grabbed the slip of paper on which I had written Isaiah's number, thinking that I might as well get it over with. I dialed his number.

"Hello?" he said, and I was surprised at how readily I could recognize his voice, which I hadn't heard in a few years.

"Hello, Isaiah. This is Patrick Madrid."

There was a long pause. "Uh. . . . Patrick, you weren't supposed to call me."

"What? Our mutual acquaintance, Robert, called yesterday specifically asking me to call you. He said you *asked* him to."

"Well, that's true," Isaiah said in a guarded voice. "When he told me he knew you, I at first thought it would be fine if you called, but then, after thinking about it awhile, I changed my mind. I didn't—and don't—want to have any kind of unpleasant confrontation with you about my decision to leave the Catholic Church and become Mormon. I got in touch with Robert and asked him to call and tell you *not* to call me."

"I never got that message," I replied, "and I wouldn't have called you if I had."

"That's all right," Isaiah said graciously. "Well, as long as we're on the phone now, let's talk."

And talk we did. For well over an hour, I tried every avenue of approach I could think of to convince him that he had made a terrible mistake in leaving the Catholic Church to become Mormon, but nothing I said made a bit

of difference. Isaiah was confident and quick with his re-
sponses to my queries. It seemed as if I were trying to stop
a tank by throwing Ping-Pong balls at it. When I hung up
the phone, I felt even more depressed and did my best to
put the whole strange scenario out of my mind.

Six months passed. One Saturday morning I got a call
from Isaiah, asking if I had time to talk. He probably wants
round two, I thought with a wan sigh of resignation.

His tone of voice was an odd mixture of joyful and brittle. "I wanted you to be the first to know that I have left
Mormonism and come home to the Catholic Church."

I didn't know how to react. I was elated at the news but
utterly mystified at how he could make what seemed to me
to be such a radical conversion away from a religion he was
so confident in the last time we spoke.

"Do you remember that question you asked me?" he
asked.

"Ha!" I snorted. "I asked you fifty questions that day!
Which one do you have in mind?"

"Well," he said in the calm, measured voice of someone
about to reveal a momentous secret, "you asked me a question that shook me to my foundations. You asked: *'Isaiah,
you are a Catholic priest. How could you turn your back on Christ
in the Eucharist?'*"

I did not recall asking him that, but *he* had been so force-
fully struck by it that, as he described it, his hands trembled
as he put the phone down after our earlier conversation.
He described how that question had irritated him. It an-
gered him. And it also never left his mind. He told me how
he couldn't stop it from ringing in his ears: *"How could I*

*turn my back on Christ in the Eucharist?"* He even related how he had once woken up out of a deep sleep with that question wrapped around his mind, not letting go.

As Isaiah told me the whole amazing story, I could hear in his voice the sorrow and pain he felt for leaving the Church as well as an exuberant, childlike joy at having found his way home again. His saga of reconversion involved a series of providential circumstances,[19] but all of them, he told me, arose only after our initial conversation. That question about the Eucharist haunted him until finally, as he described it, like a fog burning away in the light of the noonday sun, he realized with horror what a terrible mistake he had made in abandoning his Catholic faith.

Jesus, in the Holy Eucharist, had reached out from the tabernacle through Robert to me, from me through a phone line to Salt Lake City, and gently tapped this ex-priest on the shoulder, on his heart, in fact, and said, "Come home." And he did.

# 5

# The Cure for What Ails Me

## CONFESSION AND HEALING

WE ALL KNOW THAT WHEN YOU GET SERIOUSLY SICK, you need medicine. If your illness is serious enough, an operation might be necessary to cure it. Clearly, no one *likes* being on meds or going under the knife, but if that's what it takes, we do it even though doing it is painful. Our souls are no different from our bodies in that regard. By our own sins, we become spiritually sickened. God prescribes medicine that is simple, though not easy: repent and turn away from your sins (see Acts 3:19). Isaiah 1:16–20 continues on this point:

> Wash yourselves; make yourselves clean; remove the evil of your doings from before my eyes; cease to do evil, learn to do good; seek justice, correct oppression; defend the fatherless, plead for the widow. "Come now, let us reason together, says the LORD: though your sins are like scarlet, they shall be as white as snow; though

they are red like crimson, they shall become like wool.
If you are willing and obedient, you shall eat the good
of the land; but if you refuse and rebel, you shall be
devoured by the sword; for the mouth of the LORD
has spoken."

Turning away from sin is the hard part. We can become
so enslaved by pleasure, power, entertainment, money,
gadgets, and so on and have a very hard time turning away
from them in order to accept God's gift of freedom and
peace. The more wrong we do, the more likely we are to
do wrong. Only God's grace can free us from this vicious
circle.

One key reason why I am Catholic is that the Catholic
Church has the remedy for what ails me. The Church is a
hospital for sick people like you and me. We all suffer from
the malaria of sin—it's a spiritual disease that's contracted
not through the bite of a mosquito but from the bite of
an apple. Adam and Eve, by their original sin, set into motion a catastrophic chain of events, each link of which is a
sin—and my sins and yours are forged into it. Each time we
sin, each time we willfully act against God's perfect and all-
holy plan for our lives, that chain constrains us ever more
tightly. We bring remorse, misery, regrets, emptiness, and
heartache upon ourselves, even when we *know* we should
avoid doing something we know is bad for us, something
we know deep down inside isn't just harmful but wrong.

That quick hit of pleasure is exchanged for a lifetime of
negative consequences and, at least for those who die in a
state of unrepentance, an eternity of anguished separation

from God. Catholics and other Christians call this "hell." According to the *Catechism of the Catholic Church,* "The chief punishment of hell is eternal separation from God, in whom alone man can possess the life and happiness for which he was created and for which he longs." Some fifteen hundred years ago, Saint Augustine expressed it this way: "Everlasting God, in whom we live and move and have our being: You have made us for Yourself, and our hearts are restless until they rest in You." (I will return to the question of longing in chapter 10.)

The horrible reality of hell, then, for those who send themselves there by obstinately refusing God's grace, is that they will have forever deprived themselves of the one and only thing that can bring them true happiness and lasting rest and contentment: God Himself. This is why sin is much more an enemy of yours than the worst, most aggressive form of cancer. To allow the cancer of sin to ravage and eventually vanquish your soul is the greatest possible tragedy that could befall you.

Just as we would take whatever steps necessary to fight the physical cancer, to "beat it," as they say, God has given us the cure to the disease of sin. Its name? Jesus Christ, the Lord of life, whose saving death on the cross conquered all death and made it possible for us to receive grace, peace, and mercy through salvation in him. As he himself put it, "I am the way and the truth and the life. No one comes to the Father except through me" (John 14:6–7). "You will know the truth, and the truth will set you free" (John 8:32 NAB).

Christ sets us free from sin, starting with our own personal decision through faith to accept his gift of salvation, a decision we can only actually make as the result of God's free gift of grace (see Eph. 2:8–9) that enables us to do so.

The doorway to new life is the sacrament of baptism, as Jesus said, "whoever believes and is baptized will be saved" (Mark 16:16 NAB). The apostle Peter, on the Day of Pentecost, announced this truth to the vast crowd in Jerusalem that had assembled to hear the message of the Risen Christ being proclaimed by the apostles. After listening to Peter, Scripture says the people were "cut to the heart," and they asked the apostles, "Brethren, what shall we do?" And Peter said to them, "Repent, and be baptized every one of you in the name of Jesus Christ for the forgiveness of your sins; and you shall receive the gift of the Holy Spirit" (Acts 2:37–38).

Christ gave his Church other extremely powerful antidotes for when we fall into sin again, after baptism. Just as a dose of antivenom is needed to save the life of someone bitten by a poisonous snake, the spiritually lethal "bite" of the ancient Serpent, the devil, requires a dramatically more powerful antivenom to defeat its death-dealing spiritual toxins. Jesus gave us this in the sacrament of the Holy Eucharist. The antidote to the death-dealing fruit of the tree in the Garden of Eden is the fruit of the tree of Calvary.

The imagery of the two trees is striking. The first tree's fruit was lethal to the human race because of sin. The fruit of the second gives us life in Christ. This fruit, the Eucharist, is precisely what Jesus promised at the Last Supper, the night before he was crucified, when "he took bread, and when he had given thanks he broke it and gave it to them, saying, 'This is my body which is given for you. Do this in remembrance of me'" (Luke 22:19). The very next day, he gave his body for the redemption of the world and the salvation of many. And each time we receive his Body and Blood under the appearances of bread and wine in the Holy Eucharist we literally partake of the fruit of the tree of Calvary that counteracts with grace the devastating effects of sin.

Jesus wants us to live forever. And this is why I am Catholic: because he has endowed his Church, the Catholic Church, with the means that he established to impart the graces necessary to love and live the truth in this life so that, when we die, we can be happy with God forever in the life to come. As he said, "The thief comes only to steal and kill and destroy; I came that they may have life, and have it abundantly. I am the good shepherd. The good shepherd lays down his life for the sheep" (John 10:10–11).

A second and very important dimension of the reality that the Catholic Church, in its sacraments, has the awesome power of Christ working for the salvation of souls "by grace through faith" (Eph. 2:8) is the sacrament of confession. It is in this sacrament that we are also healed of our self-inflicted wounds of sin. Even just at the level of basic human psychology I have seen how healthy and life-giving, how liberating, it is to hear those blessed words of absolution spoken by Christ through the ministry of the priest: "I absolve you from your sins." I am not being flippant when I say, if you have never tried it, you really should. You have no idea what you're missing out on: the cleansing and healing power of God's grace.

I'm convinced that, with all their faults and failings, Catholics who regularly receive the sacrament of confession are perhaps the most psychologically healthy people on earth. I believe this because I know firsthand the profoundly healing effects of this sacrament. To actually *verbalize* one's sins to another human being, a fellow sinner himself, to own up and take responsibility for the evil acts one has committed, to speak them out loud, is tremendously liberating. Even more liberating is hearing the words of absolution from the priest and knowing you have been forgiven by God.[1]

The author C. S. Lewis, an Anglican who seemed very close to the Catholic Church in many respects, once wrote of how, in his youth, he was often tormented by not knowing whether God had indeed forgiven him his sins, even after he had confessed them to God. He came to see that he was relying on his feelings for a "sense" of being forgiven, and when he didn't *feel* forgiven, he worried that he wasn't forgiven. But in the sacrament of confession, God uses our sense of hearing to impart the blessed certitude of His forgiveness when we hear the priest proclaim that we have been forgiven. Christ is speaking through the priest. As Saint Paul said,

> All this is from God, who through Christ reconciled us to himself and gave us the ministry of reconciliation; that is, in Christ God was reconciling the world to himself, not counting their trespasses against them, and entrusting to us the message of reconciliation. So

we are ambassadors for Christ, *God making his appeal through us*. We beseech you on behalf of Christ, be reconciled to God. (2 Cor. 5:18–20)

For me, the sacrament of confession is a huge part of my answer to the question *Why be Catholic?* When I have sinned, I know that Christ will forgive me if I ask him to, just as he healed the leper who implored his healing (see Mark 1:40–44). This is going directly to God for forgiveness (some people mistakenly imagine that Catholics go to the priest "instead of going to God"). Just as the leper approached Christ directly, so does the Catholic in confession approach God directly for forgiveness. But just as Christ, upon healing him, commanded the leper to go into the city and show himself to the priest and then perform the sacrifice prescribed by the Law of Moses, so, too, he commands Christians to do likewise in the sacrament of confession. There we reveal our souls to the priest so that he can pronounce definitively what God has done by forgiving us. In the case of serious sin, we are thereby restored to our rightful unity with the rest of the Body of Christ.

To illustrate what I mean by that, let me tell you a true story that happened to me.

During the lunch break at a large Catholic conference where I was speaking, I was at my table signing books and chatting with attendees. Out of the corner of my eye I noticed an attractive woman in her late thirties standing off to my left. Her body language was stiff and closed off, her arms clasped firmly over her chest. She was frowning at the other people, she was frowning at my books, and she was frowning at me. I turned to her with a smile and a cheery "Hello!" completely unprepared for her reaction. She practically bit my head off! In fact, if looks could kill, I would have been a dead man.

Staring at me acidly, she said, "Don't even try it."

I blinked, flummoxed by her antagonism. "Uh . . . don't try *what?*"

"Don't try to convert me to the Catholic Church!" she snapped, pressing her arms more tightly against her chest, her pursed lips a horizon of anger. "I know that's what you do. You try to convince people to become Catholic, but it won't work with me. I *hate* the Catholic Church! I used to be Catholic, but I left a long time ago when I became a Bible-believing Christian, so don't start up with me about Catholicism, understand?"

Wow, why is she so angry? I wondered. Should I even bother trying to talk to her? Why not just shrug and walk away? I was tempted to say, "Okay. No problem. Have a nice life," but my curiosity got the better of me. Something in her defiant look made me want to stand my ground. It was probably my pride. How could I walk away from someone who challenged me so openly (and so rudely)? No, I decided, I'll press a little further and see what happens.

"Oh, really?" I said, arching my eyebrows. "You *hate* the Catholic Church? Why is that?"

"How much time do you have?" she said sarcastically, her eyes flashing with anger.

"All the time you need," I said, with a subtle undertone of sarcasm. I remember mentally rubbing my hands together and thinking, *This should be good.*

"All right," she began vehemently, "since you asked, I hate the Catholic Church because it teaches so many un-biblical doctrines about Mary and salvation and the pope and things like that. Because the Catholic Church adds its traditions of men to the Bible, teaching people to believe things Jesus did not teach. Because it keeps people in bond-age thinking they can earn their salvation. Because you Catholics worship *Mary*! And you worship the wafer! Those things go against the Bible!" Her voice was rising now, as she warmed up to the task. Truth be told, the mercury in my own emotional thermometer was rising, too. Her stri-dent tone and the just-plain-dumb claims she was spout-ing about the Catholic Church were making me angry and defensive. I had actually stopped listening to her and was really just waiting for her to stop talking so I could retort. (This, by the way, is a very bad thing to have happen in any conversation. When you stop listening and are just waiting for the other person to shut up so you can fire back, you're arguing out of anger.)

As she talked, I reached for my Bible, getting ready to crush her arguments against the Catholic Church. It was like a scene from one of those Westerns in which two tough guys are about to have a shoot-out at high noon in the mid-dle of Main Street. They throw back their jackets to reveal their six-shooters, their fingers tapping nervously on the handles as each waits for that moment when he must draw and fire. I'm embarrassed to admit I felt a bit like that as I listened to her anti-Catholic tirade and reached for my Bible.

Then, something odd and unexpected happened. When

she had finished talking and was waiting for me to respond, expecting, I'm sure, that I would push back pretty hard, I felt an almost imperceptible intuition to be quiet. Was it a grace of God nudging me ever so slightly to keep my mouth closed? I don't know. It might have been. All I know is that I felt in that instant that I needed to remain silent. So I did. A few awkward moments passed as we looked at each other. She was waiting for my comeback, and I was waiting for . . . something. I just didn't know what.

She shook her head with a clear I-don't-know-why-I'm-wasting-my-time-with-you look on her face. "So anyway, those are some of the reasons why I don't like the Catholic Church . . ." She trailed off.

Still not sure what to say or if I should say anything, another long moment hung in the air awkwardly between us before I spoke up.

I was surprised by how mildly, even gently, the words came out of my mouth: "You said you used to be Catholic. What happened? What made you leave?"

It was as if the wind had suddenly gone out of her sails. I'm sure she was expecting me to let fly with biblical arguments against what she had just said about the Catholic Church. She obviously was surprised (and, I'm sure, relieved) that I hadn't.

"Well," she said, "it's a long story."

"I have time."

"All right, I'll tell you. My name's Susan, by the way."

"Hi, Susan. I'm Patrick."

We sat down at a lunch table out of earshot of the book browsers.

She told me how she had been raised in a large, "strict" Catholic family. I remember her saying "strict" a couple of times, though she didn't ever explain what she meant by it. She went to Catholic grammar and high schools and, she said, she just believed the Catholic Church's teachings without really questioning any of it. I just listened and nodded.

Then she paused, took a deep breath, and started telling me about how, when she was eighteen, she and her boyfriend had become sexually intimate and she eventually got pregnant.

"When I found out I was pregnant, I was devastated and scared," she said in a quiet voice. Her head was down, and she was staring at her hands. "He wanted me to have an abortion . . ."

At this, she started to cry. Through her tears she spoke of how alone and afraid she felt, not knowing whom she could turn to for advice and help. It was hard for her to talk. She told me that she felt she couldn't tell her parents she was expecting a baby for fear that they would kick her out of the house and disown her. "I couldn't confide in my relatives," she said, "because I knew they would tell my parents. I was so scared."

In a last-ditch effort to get some help, she went to a Catholic church across town, rang the rectory doorbell, and asked to speak to a priest. She had no appointment, but the secretary buzzed the intercom and in a few minutes a priest came out to speak with her. She tearfully explained her predicament to him and said that her boyfriend, who was waiting for her outside in the car, had been pressuring her to have an abortion. But she didn't want to have an abortion, so she came to the rectory for advice and help.

Amazingly, he was brusque and impatient with her and said something like "Don't worry about it. These home pregnancy tests are often inaccurate. Take the test again in a few days. It's probably nothing. And by the way, I don't really have time to talk with you right now, I have other things I need to do." And with that, he dismissed her and walked back into his office. He didn't pray with her. He didn't counsel her. He didn't show any Christ-like concern for this poor young woman who was scared and alone and completely unsure what to do. The one person she turned to for help, a priest, brushed her off because he was too busy to care. She stumbled out of the rectory in tears.

"When I got into the car where my boyfriend was waiting for me, I told him what happened, and he repeated his demand that I get an abortion," she said. "I didn't see any other choice. So he drove me down to the clinic, and I got it over with."

By now, Susan was so overcome with emotion she could no longer speak. She put her head down on the table and sobbed—the deep, wrenching sobs of a sorrow so painful, so profoundly desolating that I could literally feel her aching as I sat there, saying nothing, just watching her cry. What *could* I say anyway? What could I possibly say that could alleviate her misery? I felt so utterly useless and inadequate as I sat there in an uncomfortable silence waiting for her to start talking again.

After what seemed like a very long time but what was

probably no more than a minute or two, Susan had regained her composure enough to finish telling me what happened.

"After . . . , after I had the abortion, I just *hated* myself," she whispered. "I never told my parents, and I couldn't stand it. They didn't know what I had done to my baby. They thought I was still their 'good daughter.' I couldn't live with myself. And I was so angry at that *priest!*" she added. "If only he had tried to help me! If only he had been willing to . . ." She trailed off again, that anger having crept back into her eyes. Her bitterness was palpable.

And then she said something truly amazing. More to herself than to me, she said flatly, "And then I started to hate the Catholic Church. That priest represented the Church in my mind. I was in this terrible situation because he wouldn't help me. The Catholic Church wouldn't help me! And every time I tried going to Mass I would get so furious I had to leave, so I stopped going." She added that her fundamentalist Protestant friends egged her on in this regard and encouraged her to leave the Catholic Church and join their fellowship, which she did. And for the next twenty years or so, she was bitterly anti-Catholic. Fast-forward now to the two of us sitting together in awkward silence at that table. I had absolutely no idea what to say, no clue what I could possibly offer her by way of advice or encouragement. As a man, I could only try to imagine the anguish that she as a woman must be feeling over her abortion. I knew I had to say *something*, but what?

After another long, awkward pause, I blurted out the

only thing that came to mind: "You need to go to confession."

The expression on Susan's face changed in a flash. Staring at me as if I had said, "Here, hold this rattlesnake," her eyes flashed again in anger and disbelief.

"*What!* How dare you tell me 'go to confession'? Didn't you hear what I said? I *hate* the Catholic Church. There's no way I would ever go back."

"Yes," I said, floundering, "but Jesus is waiting for you in the sacrament of confession. He wants to heal you, he *can* heal your wound from the abortion. But you need to go to him."

Pushing the chair back, she rose abruptly. "I'm sorry if I wasted your time with my story. I think I should go now."

My heart fell. I knew I had blown it. Susan was obviously irritated again, with the Catholic Church, with me. She had opened up to me, a total stranger, with her deepest, most painful secret, and I had gone and said something oafish in response. "You need to go to confession?" Why had I said that? I kicked myself for bungling this, for not having had the presence of mind to come up with something more soothing and empathetic. I fumbled my way through an apology, with the hope that she'd at least read a book or listen to a CD. She slung her purse over her shoulder with a look that said, "Well, *that* was a mistake." We shook hands politely and I wished her well. As Susan walked away, I mentally kicked myself again for having sabotaged the powerful breakthrough she had made with my inept comment about going to confession.

I did my best to forget the whole thing and had pretty much succeeded, until about six weeks later, when I got an e-mail from Susan. I gasped when I read her message: "Dear Patrick, you were right. I needed to go to confession." She related how my comment "You need to go to confession" had so irritated her that she couldn't stop thinking about it. The more she thought about it, the more irritated she became. That thought, "I need to go to confession," even woke her up out of a sound sleep one night. Eventually, she explained, she got tired of fighting this thought that doggedly pursued her and, breaking down in prayer, she told God that if it was really Him telling her to go to confession, she would, but she still didn't like the Catholic Church!

After making her decision, Susan went to a Catholic parish and made a good, sincere confession about the abortion and everything else on her heart. As she described it to me, it was as if the ice around her heart were melted by the warmth of God's grace because she knew she had finally been forgiven. The ice melted. The dam broke. And all the toxic pain of her abortion began to leave her and the healing could begin. Thanks be to God, not only did she come back to the Catholic Church, but she had her marriage blessed and was able to finally forgive the priest who had shunned her and resume a happy sacramental life in the very Church she had hated for so long, never realizing that it was not the Catholic Church that was the problem.

There are countless true stories like this of how Jesus Christ heals and transforms even the most hardened of sinners through the sacraments of the Catholic Church. These true stories of repentance and restoration have literally changed the course of history for the good through Christ's ministry of repentance, forgiveness, and hope through his Church.

I am grateful for these remedies for sin that are mine (and yours) in the sacraments. My advice to everyone, especially those whose troubled consciences nag them, is to return to the house of the Father and receive the many blessings he wants to bestow on them through the sacraments of the Church.

Come to me, all who labor and are heavy laden, and I will give you rest. Take my yoke upon you, and learn from me; for I am gentle and lowly in heart, and you will find rest for your souls. For my yoke is easy, and my burden is light. (Matt. 11:28–30)

# 6

# A Rock That Will Not Roll

## PETER AND THE PAPACY

IT'S HARD TO IMAGINE A MORE IMPROBABLE AND IN-auspicious starting point for the papacy. Of all places to launch his worldwide revolution of love, Jesus chose Capernaum, a humble fishing village of barely a thousand souls tucked away in the boondocks of Galilee, the hick northern region of Palestine. It was here, on the shore of Lake Galilee, that he handpicked the nucleus of twelve men who would become his closest disciples, soon to be known as the apostles. Among the first to be chosen was an impetuous fisherman named Simon Bar-Jona, who, the Gospels tell us, "immediately" left the toil of his nets when Jesus called to him and his brother Andrew, "Follow me, and I will make you fishers of men" (Matt. 4:19). There must have been an immensely powerful magnetism emanating from Jesus for these ten simple words to have had such an abrupt and life-changing effect on a successful businessman like Simon.

Within three years, those ten words had forever changed Simon, launching him on a daring global rescue mission he could have never imagined, one in which he carried the message of Jesus directly to the very heart of pagan Rome and died there, violently, at the hands of those he sought to convert. His martyrdom by inverted crucifixion in Nero's Circus in Rome (c. A.D. 65–67), after a quarter century of ministering there with Saint Paul, marked the beginning of the papacy as we know it: the unbroken succession of 265 men who succeeded Peter as pope, the Bishop of Rome. The historical record reveals that many of the popes were heroic and saintly, some were scoundrels, and the overwhelming majority were good men trying valiantly to carry out the difficult and often dangerous task that Christ had entrusted to Peter when he made him the chief shepherd of the Church, saying, "Feed my lambs. . . . Tend my sheep. . . . Feed my sheep" (John 21:15–17). The crucifix is an uncompromising reminder to each pope that Christ's "Follow me" is never to be separate from his teaching that "a servant is not greater than his master" (John 15:20). "I am the good shepherd," he says. "The good shepherd lays down his life for the sheep" (John 10:11). Regardless of how well or poorly any given pope lives up to that Christlike ideal, laying down his life for the Church is his single most fundamental duty.

The papacy is by far the oldest, most enduring institution in Christian history. Jesus personally established the papacy when he promised to build his Church on the rock of Peter, an indefectible, indestructible Church against which not even the gates of hell could prevail. Not surprisingly, therefore, the papacy has stood the test of time, surviving intact the onslaught of twenty centuries' worth of harassment, ridicule, bloody martyrdom, secular interference, religious opposition, wars, revolutions, internecine intrigues, and bad Catholics.

Most, though not all, of the hard, historical data we have about Simon Peter's life and times are contained in the Four Gospels and the Acts of the Apostles. He himself left us two brief New Testament epistles bearing his name, but they contain virtually no information about his own personal background and circumstances. We don't know when he was born, for example, but according to historians he died sometime between A.D. 65 and A.D. 67, in Rome, at the hands of the emperor Nero, who had unleashed a bloody persecution of the Church there. Eusebius, the fourth-century Catholic historian, recounts the circumstances of the martyrdoms of Saints Peter and Paul in Rome,[1] describing Peter as the "strongest and greatest of the apostles, and the one who on account of his virtue was the speaker for all the others."[2] His preaching won many converts to the Catholic Church, including many noble Romans and members of the imperial government and their families.

When martyrdom came for Peter,[3] he was succeeded by a series of stalwart men who served as pope. Tradition records that Linus, Anacletus, Clement I, Evaristus, and the subsequent popes also gave their lives as martyrs for the faith.[4]

Every one then who hears these words of mine and does them will be like a wise man who built his house upon the rock; and the rain fell, and the floods came, and the winds blew and beat upon that house, but it did not fall, because it had been founded on the rock.

And every one who hears these words of mine and does not do them will be like a foolish man who built his house upon the sand; and the rain fell, and the floods came, and the winds blew and beat against that house, and it fell; and great was the fall of it.

I believe it's self-evident that Christ would not give his disciples advice that he himself would not follow. It's no coincidence, therefore, that the Lord said that the wise man builds his house on an unshakable "rock," and Christ himself promises to build *his* house, the Church, on a rock—the rock of Peter:

Now when Jesus came into the district of Caesare'a Philippi, he asked his disciples, "Who do men say that the Son of man is?" And they said, "Some say John the Baptist, others say Eli'jah, and others Jeremiah or one of the prophets." He said to them, "But who do you say that I am?" Simon Peter replied, "You are the Christ, the Son of the living God." And Jesus answered him, "Blessed are you, Simon Bar-Jona! For flesh and blood has not revealed this to you, but my Father who is in heaven. And I tell you, you are Peter, and on this rock I will build my church, and the powers of death shall not

prevail against it. I will give you the keys of the kingdom of heaven, and whatever you bind on earth shall
be bound in heaven, and whatever you loose on earth
shall be loosed in heaven." (Matt. 16:13–19)

Since its earliest days, the Catholic Church understood
that Jesus Christ gave this rustic fisherman, Simon Peter,
a special prominence and authority among the apostles.
Peter was not the smartest of the Twelve, nor was he the
closest to Christ in terms of personal friendship, and he
certainly did not have any kind of training in theology, rhet-
oric, or administration (in fact, he had no training beyond
the practical know-how required to run his fishing business). And yet, the Gospels consistently show Peter to be
front and center during the Lord's three-year public ministry and beyond. Countless biblical details reveal this fact.

Simon Peter is mentioned in the Gospels at least 195
times by his various names and nicknames: Simon,[5] Peter,
Cephas,[6] Kepha, Kephas, and so on. The apostle who is
named the next most often is John, whose name appears a
mere twenty-nine times. The others are mentioned fewer
times and some, such as Bartholomew, are hardly spoken
of at all. Sometimes, we see a reference to "Peter and his
companions" and "Peter and the rest of the apostles," as
if Peter represented the entire group and by mentioning
him alone by name all had been included.[7]

In the New Testament, all twelve of the apostles are listed
by name four separate times[8] and, in each instance, Peter is
always listed first and Judas always dead last. Although this

in itself proves nothing about Peter's role as chief of the apostles, it is a significant indication of his prominence that he is always named first, especially when juxtaposed against the traitor, Judas, whose being named last is a clear sign of his ignominy and the contempt in which he has been held by Christians ever since.

This man Peter personified a perplexing combination of valor and cowardice, wisdom and brashness, faith and fear. In this he is like the vast majority of weak and selfish human beings who are called by God to great things in spite of their frailties. His limitations were no barrier to Christ's plans for him. Rather, Peter's humanity shows the power of God's grace—power that could dramatically transform a craven deserter (Mark 14:66–74) into a defender of Christ who bravely faced down the combined might of the hostile Jewish Sanhedrin (Acts 4:1–22; 5:17–42).

In the Bible, the transformative power of God's grace is sometimes denoted by a name change. Interestingly, Jesus called Simon "rock" the very first time he met him, though he wouldn't formally bestow that new name on Peter for nearly two years.

> One of the two who heard John [i.e., the Baptist] speak, and followed him, was Andrew, Simon Peter's brother. He first found his brother Simon, and said to him, "We have found the Messiah" (which means Christ). He brought him to Jesus. Jesus looked at him, and said, "So you are Simon the son of John? You shall be called Cephas" (which means Peter). (John 1:40–42)[9]

Notice that in this same context Jesus meets another disciple, Nathan'a-el, for the first time. Nathaniel utters a statement about Jesus ("Rabbi, you are the Son of God! You are the King of Israel!") that is nearly identical to what Simon would exclaim much later in Matthew 16:16: *"You are the Christ, the Son of the living God."* This shows us that Jesus wasn't just "waiting around" for someone, anyone, to get his identity right, as if the person he chose to be the rock on which he would build his Church didn't really matter, so long as he got the wording right.

No. Jesus had a plan for Peter. It was a plan so big and so unexpected (so *unlikely*, really, given Peter's lack of preparation for the task ahead) that it involved a significant name change, from Simon[10] to Peter. Simon in Hebrew is *Shim'on* and means "to hear" or "he heard." Peter is the anglicized form of the Aramaic word *kepha*, meaning "rock." Not long after receiving his new name from Christ in Matthew 16, the Aramaic version began to give way to the more commonly used Greek translation, *petros*. But the Greek word for rock is feminine, *petra*, and was thus a highly unusual choice for a man's name, especially that of a burly fisherman like Simon Bar-Jona, so it was used with a masculine ending (comparable to how the name Mary is masculinized to Mario). There is no distinction in Christ's words to Simon in Matthew 16, as some have argued, to suggest that when the Lord declared, "You are rock [*petros*] and upon this rock [*petra*] I will build my Church," he was speaking of two different rocks.[11]

Christ made Peter the first pope, the rock on which he would build his Church, his "prime minister" to whom he entrusted the "keys of the kingdom of heaven."[12] The Gospels reveal striking incidents in which Christ singles the fisherman out for particular leadership roles.

In Luke 5:3 we read that it was from Simon Peter's fishing boat that Christ preached to the crowd. The multitude was so great that, being hemmed in right at the water's edge, the Lord stepped into the boat to "put out a little from the land" so he could teach them. It is worth noting that this minor biblical detail became the source of the Church's term for itself as being the "barque of Peter"[13] from which the Gospel of Christ is transmitted to the whole world. This is an image that has long been depicted in Christian art, and its basis is found in this passage.

In Luke 22:31–32, Jesus warns Simon Peter, saying, "Simon, Simon, behold Satan has demanded to sift all of you like wheat, but I have prayed that your own faith may not fail; and once you have turned back, you must strengthen your brothers." This is a clear reference to the special leadership role Simon Peter was being entrusted with. Christ, knowing full well that the apostles would scatter like frightened sheep once their shepherd had been struck down, appointed Peter the chief of the apostles whose role would be indispensable in rallying them and pulling them back together into a cohesive, functioning group.

Peter's leadership role was reaffirmed and emphasized after Christ's Resurrection when Jesus asked him three times, "Simon, do you love me?" (likely as a way of symbolically annulling Peter's threefold denial of the Lord foretold by Jesus in Matthew 26:33–35).[14] Each time Peter responded with, "Yes, Lord, you know that I love you,"

Christ said, "Feed my lambs." This is another important biblical monument to Peter's special status and primacy among the apostles. Christ had conferred upon him the role of chief shepherd, a role that all the Church Fathers who comment on this issue verify was the firm belief and teaching of the early Church.[15]

On Easter Sunday, we see Peter and John run frantically to inspect Christ's empty tomb. The Gospel account tells us that John (who was younger and evidently more alacritous than Peter), though he arrived at the entrance to the tomb first, paused and waited for Peter to arrive and enter ahead of him. Although this detail can be easily passed over without recognizing its importance, it suggests that John had a respectful deference for Peter.

Acts 1:12–26 tells us that it was Peter who rallied the other apostles to cast lots to choose a successor for the suicide Judas. From that day forward, Matthias was "enrolled with the eleven Apostles."

On the Day of Pentecost, Simon Peter led the apostles in preaching the Good News of the Risen Christ to the inhabitants of Jerusalem (Acts 2). It was he who performed the first post-Resurrection miracle in Acts 3, and in Acts 10 it is to Peter alone among the apostles that God reveals the teaching that Gentiles did not have to become Jews first in order to convert to Christianity. Later, at the Council of Jerusalem, it is Peter who delivers this revelation to the Church (Acts 15). In Galatians 1:18, Saint Paul mentions that, after his own dramatic conversion to Christ, followed by a lengthy period of prayer and preparation, he did not embark on his apostolic ministry before he first went up to

Jerusalem to confer with Peter, with whom he remained for two weeks. This is a clear indication that Saint Paul himself recognized that Peter had a special role as leader that even he had to acknowledge.

I could list here many other biblical examples that point to Peter's primacy among the apostles, but I'll simply conclude with a thought drawn from my book *Pope Fiction: Answers to 30 Myths and Misconceptions About the Papacy*:

Peter strides through the first fifteen chapters of Acts performing miracles, rebuking the high and mighty who oppose Christ, personally welcoming the converted Saul into the Church, planting churches that flourish even to this day, receiving revelation from heaven, teaching, admonishing, encouraging and leading. Decades later, when his supreme hour finally arrived, he fulfilled Christ's prophecy about him: "When you are old, you will stretch out your hands, and someone will lead you where you do not want to go" (John 21:18).

In A.D. 65, Simon Peter was arrested in Rome by the pagan authorities for the crime of being a Christian. He was bound and led by soldiers to Nero's Circus. There, he was nailed upside-down to a cross and left to die. Afterward, his body was hauled a few hundred feet away and thrown into a shallow grave. No one at that moment could have known that on that site, over that forlorn and abandoned corpse, would be raised the universal focal point of the Christian religion: St. Peter's Basilica and the Vatican.[16]

From that bleak day when Peter was put to death by Nero and, "though condemned in the flesh in human estimation, [he] might live in the spirit in the estimation of God" (1 Pet. 4:6, NAB), his influence as the Prince of the apostles never waned in the Church. In fact, the bishops of Rome, some 266 of them from Peter all the way down to Pope Francis, have been living links in an unbroken chain of apostolic succession stretching from the brash Galilean fisherman down to the abstemious and laid-back Argentinian Jesuit who today occupies the chair of Peter.

One of the most significant aspects of the papacy is the Catholic doctrine of infallibility, a teaching that is, unfortunately, widely misunderstood, even by many Catholics. Infallibility is explained at length in paragraphs 889–92 of the *Catechism of the Catholic Church,* but I can boil it down for you.

First, notice that Christ made some heavy-duty promises to Peter and the apostles:

- "He who listens to you listens to me, and he who rejects you rejects me" (Luke 10:16). "Whoever listens to you listens to me. Whoever rejects you rejects me. And whoever rejects me rejects the one who sent me" (NAB).
- "When the Spirit of truth comes, he will guide you into all the truth" (John 16:13).
- "All authority in heaven and on earth has been given to me. Go therefore and make disciples of all

nations, baptizing them in the name of the Father
and of the Son and of the Holy Spirit, teaching
them to observe all that I have commanded you;
and lo, I am with you always, to the close of the age"
(Matt. 28:18–20).

These clearly are grants of a special, binding teaching
authority. When the apostles taught, the early Christians
couldn't simply ignore teachings they didn't like or hive
off and start their own "church" where they interpreted
Christ's teachings in a way other than how the apostles interpreted them. Even so, there were some who attempted
to do just that, as Saint Paul specifically warned about in
1 Timothy 1:3–7.

Infallibility is a necessary consequence of Christ's promise that when the apostles taught it was really he himself
who was teaching through them, because if Christ literally
meant "he who hears you hears me," then he put himself
in the position of having to ratify what the apostles taught.
But what if they were to teach error? What if, say, Peter had
started preaching that Jesus was a great man but not really
God? How could Christ ratify such an error? He could
not have, of course. And this is why the Catholic Church
teaches that the gift of infallibility necessarily flows from
Christ's gift of this special teaching authority.

Infallibility is a special charism, a spiritual gift given by
Jesus Christ to his Church, by which the appointed teachers
of the faith (i.e., the pope and all the bishops of the Catholic Church in union with him) are prevented from formally
teaching error in the areas of faith and morals.[17]

The pope has this charism individually by virtue of his office, and the other bishops of the Church possess it corporately and exercise it whenever they participate in an ecumenical council.[18] Here's how I have explained papal infallibility elsewhere, what it is and what it isn't:

> Infallibility doesn't mean that the pope is prompted by God to do or teach something. It doesn't even guarantee that the pope, when he does teach, will be as effective or persuasive or clear as he should be in what he teaches.
>
> Papal infallibility . . . is a guarantee that God the Holy Spirit will preserve the pope from formally teaching error.
>
> Much like a steel guardrail that lines the outer edge of a twisty mountain road, put there to keep cars from going over a cliff, the gift of papal infallibility is a divine protection against the catastrophe of the Church careening over the precipice of heresy, even if the pope were to drive recklessly, or, as it were, to fall asleep at the wheel.[19]

Catholic teaching on papal infallibility has nothing to do with personal behavior. Even the greatest, holiest saints were not infallible (i.e., those were not popes), and every single one of the popes, including those who were terrible sinners, were infallible. Here's how that works. Infallibility does not mean *impeccability*, which is freedom from sin. All popes, even the saintly ones, have been sinners. The pope's personal behavior is not in question here. A given pope could be a scoundrel and yet he would still have the protection of infallibility—the Holy Spirit would restrain him from teaching error to the Church in spite of (better yet, *because of*) his immorality.

To say that the world today is "complex" and "dangerous" is a major understatement. True, every generation has been prone to see itself as having the worst of it, but I believe there are a number of societal malignancies rampant right now in the early twenty-first century that defy comparison with the problems of any earlier era in scope, magnitude, and sheer destructive power. These malignancies include a rapid and radical shift away from what have become scornfully known as "traditional values" in favor of aggressively secular mores that revel in things like "gay marriage," divorce, pornography, assisted suicide ("mercy killing"), abortion, and contraception. We are witnessing the implacable rise of militant atheism, global terrorism, and a vast and steadily proliferating government-controlled surveillance system that silently monitors, records, and archives a permanent digital chronicle of our daily public and "private" activities. Ominously, the ever more finely tuned capabilities of this high-tech surveillance system seems poised to be capable of exerting draconian controls over the lives of individual people with the flick of a switch. Conspiracy theories abound as to who exactly have their hands on those switches, and I have no wish to enter into that fever swamp of speculation. But it is beyond clear that the world today, especially technologically, is dramatically different from that of any previous generation. The generalized, worldwide abandonment of Christian moral principles is in full slide, and there seems little reason to think that we moderns will be able to shake off our addictions to entertainment, pleasure, material possessions, gadgets, pornography, and intellectual laziness.

Things have gotten so chaotic and precarious that it's as if Saint Paul were writing about this very generation when he warned:

> But understand this, that in the last days there will come times of stress. For men will be lovers of self, lovers of money, proud, arrogant, abusive, disobedient to their parents, ungrateful, unholy, inhuman, implacable, slanderers, profligates, fierce, haters of good, treacherous, reckless, swollen with conceit, lovers of pleasure rather than lovers of God, holding the form of religion but denying the power of it. (2 Tim. 3:1–5)

Perhaps he was speaking of this generation.

All I know is that our culture seems to be plunging headlong into a fearful storm of civil strife, a collapsing global economy, evil ideologies run amok, and a metastasizing tendency toward totalitarianism, which always seems to be lurking in the shadows, ready to exploit opportunities presented by social upheaval and pandemonium. Jesus, though, has other plans for this world. He established the Catholic Church on the rock of Peter precisely so that it would be able to ride out even the worst of the storms without being dislodged, knocked down, or swept away.

When I'm asked why I am Catholic, one of my answers is "because of the papacy, the rock on which Christ is building his Church." The way I figure it, I should trust the Lord's promises and stand squarely on that rock, not to the left of it or to the right of it, not in front of it or behind it, but *on* it. If I am with the pope, I know I am with Christ. And if I am with Christ, come hell or high water, I will not be swept away by whatever the storm might throw.

The papacy has always been a sign of contradiction. Because the papacy is one of the most prominent and visible images of the Catholic Church, it inevitably attracts controversy, opposition, harassment, and even persecution. Some contradict this truth by saying that Jesus was not God, so none of that matters anyway. Others argue that while Jesus did say this, he did not mean that *Peter* was the rock on which he would build his Church.[20] Still others, who care nothing one way or the other about the divinity of Christ or the controversy about who or what is the "rock" mentioned in Matthew 16, oppose the papacy because it so iconically represents the Catholic Church, and they are against the Catholic Church.

The reasons for this opposition vary, but if the two-thousand-year history of the Catholic Church has proved anything, it is that the papacy has always been the bull's-eye on the target for those who dislike, gainsay, and otherwise oppose the Catholic Church. If Christ established the papacy, then the Catholic Church is the one true Church. And if it could be shown that the papacy is a sham, not established or sanctioned by Christ, a medieval corruption introduced by religious charlatans in their desire to amass wealth, power, and influence, then the Catholic Church would thereby be shown to be false as well.

The papacy as a sign of contradiction can also be understood as a juxtaposition between the holiness of the office and the sometimes wicked men who have held that office. This concept can seem incredibly counterintuitive, as we wonder why Christ would entrust such an important and holy ministry to unworthy men. The answer, I believe, is seen in the fact that he chose twelve men to be his apostles, and all of them were flawed. Judas betrayed him, Peter denied knowing him, and all of them, with the exception of Saint John, ran away from him when he was captured and put on trial for his life. Even before that crisis, the Gospels show us the apostles as a group of doubting,[21] vacillating,[22] bickering,[23] hard-hearted,[24] wannabe leaders. Indeed, the Twelve were themselves gigantic signs of contradiction. What heavenly treasures Christ reposed in those ordinary men, with their weaknesses and foibles! This is why Saint Paul could exclaim, "We have this treasure in earthen vessels, to show that the transcendent power belongs to God and not to us" (2 Cor. 4:7). That is perhaps the best possible way of explaining how and why the papacy works. It is God's grace from beginning to end, building upon, holding together, and strengthening the fragile, rickety human nature and personalities of every single pope down through the ages, from Peter to Francis.

In mid-January 1995, my oldest son, Jonathon, and I flew from Los Angeles to the Philippines to oversee Catholic

Answers'[25] evangelization efforts for World Youth Day in Manila. Over 5 million people jammed the city's center that week to see and hear Pope John Paul II speak to them about the love of Jesus Christ.

But not everybody who planned to attend the event loved the pope. A team of Muslim terrorists had come to town to assassinate John Paul II in what would become known as the Bojinka plot, part of which involved one of the terrorists, disguised as a Catholic priest, getting within a few feet of the pope and then detonating a powerful bomb.

Their devilish plan would almost certainly have succeeded had it not been accidentally thwarted, only days before the pope's arrival, by a fire that swept through the terrorists' squalid apartment, caused by a chemical-mixing mishap in the kitchen. Sifting through the burned-out rooms, investigators quickly realized that the terrorists had not only been planning to kill the pope but were also putting the finishing touches on a dozen tiny, virtually undetectable "micro bombs" with which they intended to destroy many U.S. commercial airliners in midflight over the Pacific Ocean.[26]

I shudder at the thought of the carnage and grief that would have ensued had this heinous plot not been foiled, and I marvel at the realization that I would have been literally *right there* in the midst of such an unthinkable tragedy. Thanks be to God, Pope John Paul II made it safely back home to the Vatican.[27]

Was the seemingly accidental disruption of the terrorist plot mere chance? Or was there, perhaps, a divine intervention that protected the pope from the evil designs of those who sought to murder him? I am inclined to think there was just such an intervention, not because it would have been unthinkable that a pope might be killed by his enemies—that has happened many times before—but because the Lord did not will to allow those evil men to succeed in their evil intentions:

> *Deliver me from my enemies, O my God,*
> *protect me from those who rise up against me,*
> *deliver me from those who work evil,*
> *and save me from bloodthirsty men.*
>
> *For, lo, they lie in wait for my life;*
> *fierce men band themselves against me. (Ps. 59:1–3)*

Over the last two thousand years, countless tyrants, dictators, kings, politicians, and terrorists have discovered the futility of trying to destroy the papacy. Believe me, that project has been attempted over and over and over again with the same predictable results. Nada. It is true, of course, that more than a few popes have died a martyr's death, but history shows that not a single concerted effort to conquer and subdue the Catholic Church by overthrowing the pope, or imprisoning him, or even killing him has ever panned out.

Tyrants have come and gone, empires have risen and fallen, and terrorists may thrive for a time before going up in smoke, but the papacy remains intact and in place, miraculously impervious (in my opinion) to every futile attempt to destroy it. I once heard someone describe that kind of futility as like "trying to bounce on a trampoline of cement."

The atheist Soviet dictator Joseph Stalin famously scoffed, "The Pope! How many divisions has *he* got?" Well, none, to be exact. The pope does not need military troops to carry out the mission of the Church. What he needs are men and women who love God and their neighbor enough to become, as Saint Paul describes them, a "good soldier of Christ Jesus" (2 Tim. 2:3) who will don the "full armor of God" (Eph. 6:10) and "fight the good fight" (1 Tim. 6:12) with the weapons of the spirit that "are not the weapons of the world but have the power to destroy strongholds" (2 Cor. 10:4).

Stalin also boasted, "There are no fortresses that Bolsheviks cannot storm." That may have been true of the many countries the Soviet Union gobbled up along the way as it strove for world domination, but it certainly was not true of the Catholic Church in general or the papacy in particular, both of which were high-priority targets of the Russian Communists and their proxies.[28] But this was nothing new. From its earliest years, the Catholic Church and the papacy have always been seen as public enemy number one for countless emperors, kings, tyrants, presidents, prime ministers, dictators, politburos, terrorist organizations, and the like. They have all come and gone, and the Catholic Church and the papacy are still here.

Saint Peter was himself hounded and hunted, first in Palestine by Herod Agrippa (from whose dungeon he was miraculously freed [see Acts 12:5–17]), and later, after he went to minister in Italy, by the Roman authorities. He was eventually captured, imprisoned, and executed.[29]

Henceforth, the papacy remained a focal point for anti-Christian opposition and, not infrequently, persecution, and martyrdom.[30] Toward the end of the second century, Irenaeus of Lyons (who would be martyred and become a saint)[31] compiled a running list of all the bishops of Rome, from Peter to Eleutherius (d. 189), as part of an apologetics refutation of those who argued that the bishops of the Catholic Church could not trace themselves back to the apostles:

> It is within the power of all, therefore, in every church, who may wish to see the truth, to contemplate clearly the tradition of the Apostles manifested throughout the whole world; and we are in a position to reckon up those who were by the apostles instituted bishops in the Churches, and [to demonstrate] the succession of these men to our own times. . . . Since, however, it would be very tedious, in such a volume as this, to reckon up the successions of all the Churches . . . [I will demonstrate] that tradition derived from the Apostles, *of the very great, the very ancient, and universally known Church founded and organized at Rome by the two most glorious apostles, Peter and Paul;* as also [by pointing out] the faith preached to men, which comes down to our time by means of the successions of the bishops. For it is a matter of necessity that every Church should agree with *this* Church, on account of its preeminent

authority, that is, the faithful everywhere, inasmuch as the tradition has been preserved continuously by those [faithful men] who exist everywhere (emphasis added).[32]

This passage from Irenaeus is but one of many examples that could be brought forth from the testimony of the early Christians to show that they were keenly aware of and placed tremendous importance upon the role of the papacy. Contrary to what some imagine, the papacy was not a medieval invention of the Catholic Church after the Roman emperor Constantine legalized Christianity in 313 with his Edict of Milan. In fact, during the late first century, when the apostle John was still alive, we have explicit evidence that the Bishop of Rome, Pope Clement I, exercised jurisdiction over the Church at Corinth. In his well-known *First Epistle to the Corinthians*,[33] Clement gently but firmly rebukes them for having deposed a lawful bishop, as well as for sanctioning certain factions and rivalries in their midst.

Clement understood that he had a special authority to intervene in the internal affairs of another preeminent church:

If, however, any shall disobey the words *spoken by Him through us*, let them know that they will involve themselves in transgression and serious danger.[34]

Joy and gladness will you afford us, *if you become obedient to the words written by us and through the Holy Spirit* root out the lawless wrath of your jealousy according to the intercession which we have made for peace and unity in this letter (emphasis added).[35]

What's even more significant is the fact that the Corinthian Church not only received Pope Clement's instruction with docility (a strange reaction indeed if, in fact, Clement had no recognized authority beyond the boundaries of his own church at Rome) but revered his letter so highly that they assumed it was part of the inspired writings of what would become known as the New Testament. The older edition of *The Catholic Encyclopedia* says:

> The *Epistle* is in the name of the Church of Rome but the early authorities always ascribe it to Clement. Dionysius, Bishop of Corinth, wrote c. 170 to the Romans in Pope Soter's time: "Today we kept the holy day, the Lord's day, and on it we read your letter—and we shall ever have it to give us instruction, even as the former one written through Clement." (Eusebius, *Church History* IV.30)[36]

I was eighteen in 1978 when Cardinal Karol Wojtyla was elected the 264th pope, and I clearly remember the shock and anticipation everyone felt when it was announced that we had a Polish pope. The Catholic Church was then still in the depths of the liturgical confusion and craziness that seemed to have swept over every parish like a dust storm. Many priests and nuns had abandoned their vocations in the preceding decade. Laypeople were woefully uncatechized, and many even *anti*catechized by those who preached serious errors in the name of the ever-ambiguous, though pleasant-sounding "spirit of Vatican II." The use of contraception among married Catholic couples (not to mention singles) skyrocketed, Mass attendance and vocations plummeted, and the Catholic Church in America became more or less mired in the morass of a bland, beige, innocuous caricature of its former self. A culture of dissent from Catholic teaching was prevalent, resulting in an effete American Catholicism that had lost its way every bit as much as it had lost its vigor.[37]

The inertia began to dissipate when Pope John Paul II stepped into the picture. It didn't change immediately, nor did his long pontificate (twenty-six and a half years) correct all, or even most, of the problems and malaise Catholicism faced in the West, but he did do a tremendous amount of good, nudging the Catholic Church back on course. His indefatigable willingness to travel to foreign countries, bringing the Gospel of Jesus personally to countless millions of Catholics and non-Catholics around the world, was impressive. It commanded attention. *He* commanded attention, even from dictators, atheists, and playboy presidents. He personally helped bring down the Iron Curtain and topple the godless Communist Soviet Union.[38] Pope John Paul II was certainly not perfect, no pope has been, but he was a great man with a powerful intellect and a voracious desire to speak about Jesus Christ and his Blessed Mother to a world that desperately needs hope and peace, and to a faltering Catholic Church that badly needed to be picked up, dusted off, and cheered up. This he did well and faithfully to the end of his days. It is no surprise to me that was canonized a saint on April 27, 2014.

For me, the papacy with all its ups and downs, dark chapters and bright triumphs, is strong proof that the Catholic Church was established by Christ: it has remained intact and vital for nearly two thousand years in spite of every challenge that has come against it, including that of bad popes, weak popes, and incompetent popes. But I thank God for the many good and holy popes the Church has been blessed with, up to and including Blessed John Paul II, Benedict XVI, and Francis. They are good men doing a crushingly difficult and perilous job, and from beginning to end, it is the power of Christ that bears them up, just as he bore Simon Peter up as he swung his legs out over the side of the fishing boat and miraculously began to walk on water. It is Christ who preserves the Catholic Church. And the pope, as the Vicar of Christ and the visible head of the Church on earth (Christ is *the* head of the Church; see Eph. 5:23), is a real and present reminder, a symbol that is more than just a symbol, of Christ's desire that Peter continue to "feed my sheep."

In 1992, I was in Rome with a colleague for a week of meetings with various Vatican officials in order to acquaint them with the work of Catholic Answers. Through the auspices of a curial archbishop with whom we had dinner one evening, we were able to obtain an invitation to attend John Paul II's morning Mass in his private chapel in the Vatican. As Mass began and he processed past me on his way toward the altar, we locked eyes for an instant. It meant nothing to him, of course; I was just another of the countless pilgrims he had encountered during his long and fruitful pontificate. But for me, the moment was electric. I was struck by how fatigued he looked, even then, before the ravages of his Parkinson's disease began to manifest themselves. The deep lines of worry and labor on his face bespoke the strain of his office as much as the exigencies of old age. His eyes, too, though tired, flashed with the spark of love—the love of a harried father whose large and rowdy family with all its problems and needs keeps him up at night with prayer and worry.

It was an awesome experience to be in his presence, just a short distance away, knowing that here was a successor of Peter, a living link in the two-thousand-year chain of popes that has stretched, sometimes very near the breaking point, across a vast and varied expanse of human history, across dark epochs of bloody persecution of the Church, across glorious achievements in learning and civilization, through tangled intrigues and confusing times, all the way down to that very moment when I stood in the pope's chapel as he celebrated Mass. This 264th successor of Peter was literally doing the very thing that Peter himself had heard the Lord Jesus Christ command at the Last Supper when he uttered the words "Do this in memory of me."

# 7

# Mamma Mia!

## The Blessed Virgin Mary's Role in God's Plan of Salvation

WE ARE ALL DRIVEN TOWARD GOODNESS AND BEAUTY. Beauty attracts the human heart with a gravitational pull all its own, drawing us toward it because we instinctively value beauty for its own sake. Saint Augustine wrote that "love is the beauty of the soul," meaning that the more we love God and those around us, the more truly beautiful we become. The same is true of the ineffable beauty of the Blessed Virgin Mary, God's masterpiece. For two thousand years the Catholic Church has, without apology, honored and venerated her as an important part of God's plan of salvation.

Mary is much like the stained-glass windows in a beautiful old cathedral: When viewed from the inside, with sunlight streaming through them, the windows are bright and beautiful, explosions of color that are full of meaning. But when viewed from the *outside*, these same windows can appear dark and drab, devoid of color, and unintelligible. The role of Mary in the Catholic Church can seem just like those windows when viewed from the wrong direction. For many, the Catholic emphasis on her seems superfluous, irrelevant, and even downright objectionable because it all seems to detract somehow from the love and honor we owe to God.

As a Catholic, however, I believe Mary is my mother. I am devoted to her because of who she is—the Mother of God—and because of who I want to be—like her son, Jesus. I honor her because I see that God honored her first. I love her because God loved her so much that He chose her to be the human "portal" through which He came into the world as the incarnate Word made flesh. And I implore her maternal intercession because God made her a powerful intercessor, and because I am a sinner in great need of His grace and mercy. As Pope Benedict XVI observed, "Mary's greatness consists in the fact that she wants to magnify *God*, not herself."[1] In her Magnificat prayer, she points us steadfastly to God and His greatness while also humbly acknowledging His great gifts to her:

> *My soul magnifies the Lord,*
> *and my spirit rejoices in God my Savior,*
> *for he has regarded the low estate of his handmaiden.*
> *For behold, henceforth all generations will call me*
>     *blessed;*
> *for he who is mighty has done great things for me,*
> *and holy is his name. (Luke 1:46–49)*

This prophecy, "all generations will call me blessed," is the biblical basis for the Catholic custom of referring to the Mother of the Lord as "the Blessed Virgin Mary."

I am Catholic, in part, because the Church proclaims the truth about the Blessed Virgin Mary's important and glorious role in God's plan of salvation. She is the very first Christian (the angel Gabriel brought the Good News of salvation to her first, among all other human beings). She was the first human being to accept Jesus Christ into her heart as her personal Lord and Savior. What's more, by accepting God's will for her, she assented to become the Mother of the Son of God and thereby *received* the unborn Lord Jesus Christ into her very body.

Practically alone among all other Christian groups, the Catholic Church teaches the unique role of the Blessed Virgin Mary in God's plan of salvation. The heart of this teaching is, first, that because God so loved the world, He gave His only-begotten son, that whoever believes in Him should not perish but have eternal life. And second, He sent His son into the world *through* Mary, the human "portal" between eternity and time, the living doorway through which God Himself entered this world to save it. Mary is the woman foretold in Genesis 3:15 who, by her "yes" to God's plan of salvation (see Luke 1:26–38), conceived by the Holy Spirit and gave birth to the Messiah, the Redeemer of the world. He is the one who "bruises"[2] (the head of Satan (Gen. 3:15). God sovereignly chose her to be the woman who by her "yes" would undo the terrible consequences of the first woman's, Eve's, "no" to God's will. As such, it was fitting (though by no means necessary) that God lavished her with a plentitude of graces that displayed and reflected His own glory, fitting precisely because He chose her to be the mother of Jesus Christ, true God and true man. This is why the Catholic Church honors the Blessed Virgin Mary as the "Mother of God." For as the Council of Ephesus declared in A.D. 431, she did not give birth to Christ's human nature, but to the Divine Person, the Second Person of the Blessed Trinity, who took a human nature at the Incarnation.

> In the beginning was the Word, and the Word was with God, and the Word was God. He was in the beginning with God; all things were made through him, and without him was not anything made that was made. In him was life, and the life was the light of men. The light shines in the darkness, and the darkness has not overcome it. . . . And the Word became flesh and dwelt among us, full of grace and truth; we have beheld his glory, glory as of the only Son from the Father. (John 1:1–5, 14)

But, like stained-glass windows seen from the outside, many of these aspects of the Blessed Virgin Mary that seem so obvious and understandable to Catholics can be quite difficult and even repellent to many non-Catholics. More than a few converts have told me that the Catholic Church's Marian teachings—her Immaculate Conception (sinlessness), perpetual virginity (she had no children other than Jesus), her bodily Assumption into heaven, and her role as an intercessor in heaven, to name four of the major ones—were among the most vexing and difficult for them to accept as they groped their way toward the door of the Church. One convert, a former Calvinist, once told me partly in jest that the three biggest hurdles for her were "Mary, Mary, and Mary."

Over the past twenty-seven years that I've been working in the field of Catholic apologetics, I've encountered a variety of objections to Catholic Marian teachings and have done my best to research those objections to see if, perhaps, I had been duped by the Catholic Church into believing false doctrines. I searched Scripture and scoured the writings of the Church Fathers in search of the truth about Mary. If it became clear that the Catholic Church was wrong about *this,* I reasoned, I'd walk away from it and never look back.

During my Golden Summer, when Christie's dad was badgering me about pretty much every Catholic doctrine, especially those pertaining to Mary, I began my search for answers using, first, the Bible, as well as the writings of the Church Fathers. I eventually discovered extremely helpful and enlightening books, such as William Jurgens's three-volume *The Faith of the Early Fathers,*[3] Hilda Graef's *Mary: A History of Doctrine and Devotion,*[4] and later, Luigi Gambero's *Mary and the Fathers of the Church,*[5] that were very helpful in showing the wide and deep reverence for Mary that existed universally in the early Church. This rich biblical and patristic testimony to the ancient Catholic emphasis on Mary's important role in God's plan of salvation is aptly summarized by the *Catechism of the Catholic Church,* which says of Mary that by her complete adherence to the Father's will, to his Son's redemptive work, and to every prompting of the Holy Spirit, the Virgin Mary is the Church's model of faith and charity. Thus she is a "preeminent and . . . wholly unique member of the Church"; indeed, she is the "exemplary realization" [type] of the Church.

Her role in relation to the Church and to all humanity goes still further. "In a wholly singular way she cooperated by her obedience, faith, hope, and burning charity in the Savior's work of restoring supernatural life to souls. For this reason she is a mother to us in the order of grace."[6]

Mary's *obedience* to God, her "yes" to His plan, was the grace-filled response necessary to counteract the catastrophe set in motion by Eve's disobedience in the Garden of Eden when, by eating the forbidden fruit and coaxing Adam, her husband, to do so as well, she defied God's command: "You may freely eat of every tree of the garden; but of the tree of knowledge of good and evil you shall not eat, for in the day that you eat of it you shall die" (Gen. 2:16–17). Mary's unreserved "yes" to God's request is the most powerful emblem possible to signify what all Christians are called to do, and it reminds us that God respects our freedom (He created us to be free to love) and will not trample us. His gift of grace is a *gift,* not an imposition or an implacable demand made on us. And each Christian, whether he or she realizes it, becomes like Mary when he or she freely accepts God's free gift of grace. This is a key reason the Catholic Church regards Mary as "preeminent" among Christians, for she is the very pattern and example of what it means to say "yes" to God's love.

The Catholic Church teaches that Mary's motherhood extends to all Christians because Christians are members of the *Body of Christ*[7]—a literal, not figurative, statement—and, therefore, when this mother beholds her son, she also beholds with love and solicitude all who are members of her son's mystical body. These and other truths about Mary have been a source of deep biblical and theological reflection in the Catholic Church for nearly two thousand years, expressed so powerfully in her liturgies, prayers, artwork, music, and even architecture. When we render to Mary the high honor that she is due, we further honor, adore, and praise God who first adorned her with such great glory. Which is to say that, by honoring Mary, the Catholic Church is obedient to the Bible, which teaches us to give "respect to whom respect is due, honor to whom honor is due" (Rom. 13:7).

All of these things were impressed upon me by my parents and other family members from the time I was a child. The images of the Blessed Virgin Mary in our home, praying the rosary as a family, and her special place in the liturgical life of the Catholic Church of my upbringing all helped to imprint an indelible love and appreciation for Mary on me. These were not forced upon me, any more than a family's tender affection for a beloved grandfather or grandmother is "forced" upon a child. It is a good and natural dimension of any healthy family to show love, honor, and respect to elders. And if that elder happened to be *the Mother of God*, then it's self-evident that such loving reverence would be all the more pronounced. That's how it was for me as a kid. And, looking back, I am grateful to my parents for teaching me these things.

Growing up in a devout Catholic family was, for me, deeply connected with Marian piety, at the heart of which was praying the family rosary. My parents made sure that we prayed the rosary every day when possible. To be candid, I must admit that, as a kid, I thought the rosary was kind of boring. I understood it and knew that praying its Glorious, Joyful, and Sorrowful mysteries (i.e., biblical meditations on pivotal events in the life of Christ, for all of which Mary herself was present) is a way to draw closer to God by invoking Mary's intercession. I remember once, when I was about thirteen, reading for the first time the biography of Saint Dominic Savio (1842–1857), an Italian lad who had a deep, lifelong devotion to the Blessed Virgin Mary. Because I found him to be such a compelling and heroic figure, I wanted to emulate him, love God more, and have a deeper devotion to Mary like he had.[8] My introduction to Dominic Savio was, I think, the beginning of a more pronounced and heartfelt love for Mary that has only grown and matured in me ever since. I'll say more about him shortly. Praying the rosary is an integral part of my daily prayer life.

Saint Pope John Paul II explained the rosary this way:

Meditation on the mysteries of Christ is proposed in the Rosary by means of a method designed to assist in their assimilation. It is a method *based on repetition.* This applies above all to the *Hail Mary,* repeated ten times in each mystery. If this repetition is considered super-ficially, there could be a temptation to see the Rosary as a dry and boring exercise. It is quite another thing, however, when the Rosary is thought of as an outpour-ing of that love which tirelessly returns to the person loved with expressions similar in their content but ever fresh in terms of the feeling pervading them (empha-sis added).[9]

One thing my parents instilled in us was a realization that the rosary should never be a "mechanical" prayer, re-cited clickety-clack with no thought given to what we were saying. Although I don't recall them ever actually quoting from the Bible Jesus's disapproving words about "vain rep-etition" in prayer, they definitely took pains to explain to us that when praying the rosary we should be concentrating on the biblical episode associated with each mystery: the Resurrection, the Ascension, the Finding in the Temple, the Crucifixion, and so forth. Whenever Christie's dad crit-icized the Catholic practice of using formulaic prayers, he would challenge me with Matthew 6:7–8: "And in praying do not heap up empty phrases as the Gentiles do; for they think that they will be heard for their many words. Do not be like them, for your Father knows what you need before you ask him."

His appeal to this verse "against the rosary" didn't put a dent in me or cause me any concern, because I already knew that the "vain repetition" Christ condemns here is vain precisely because, for one thing, the "gods" the pagans prayed to didn't exist, so, no matter how many litanies of grandiose titles they might call out to Zeus or Apollo or Diana, those gods were not there to hear them, anyway. Another reason is that, immediately after condemning vain repetition, the Lord proceeds to say by way of contrast, "Pray then like this . . ." and teaches the disciples the greatest of all repetitious prayers: the Our Father (Matt. 6:9–13).[10]

Two stories that I believe are interconnected resonate in my own heart and mind as indicative of the deep love the Blessed Virgin Mary has both for people in general and for me in particular. The encounters with her detailed below connect an obscure Indian man who lived in the Aztec city of Tenochtitlán (modern-day Mexico City) five hundred years ago with me, when I visited the same place on August 31, 1986. What happened (and what did *not* happen) made a profound and indelible impression on me.

## The Woman at Tepeyac

During the eleven years after the notorious Spanish conquistador Hernán Cortés vanquished the Aztec empire in central Mexico in 1520, very few Indians converted to the Catholic faith, despite the efforts of Franciscan missionaries. But in December 1531, the Blessed Virgin Mary appeared several times to a forty-seven-year-old Nahuatl Indian peasant named Juan Diego[11] on the mountainous outskirts of Tenochtitlán. Largely as a result of these apparitions, more than *11 million* Indians enthusiastically converted to the Catholic Church. They did not feel co-erced; rather, they had complete confidence in the Gospel of Jesus Christ.

On the frosty morning of December 9, 1531, the humble Indian peasant Juan Diego made his way to Mass. He heard a young woman's voice call his name several times and though he looked around, he could see no one. Then, hearing his name called again, he went farther up the path and encountered a young woman enveloped in golden light. Speaking the Nahuatl language, she identified herself to Juan Diego, saying:

> I am the Perfect Ever Virgin Holy Mary, mother of the one great God of truth who gives us life, the inventor and creator of people, the owner and lord of what is around us and what is touching us or very close to us, the owner and Lord of the sky, the owner of the earth.[12]

A contemporary account of this vision describes what Juan Diego saw:

> When he reached where she was, he was filled with admiration for the way her perfect grandeur exceeded all imagination: her clothing was shining like the sun, as if it were sending out waves of light, and the stone, the crag on which she stood, seemed to be giving out rays. Her radiance was like precious stones. It seemed like an exquisite bracelet (it seemed beautiful beyond anything else). The earth seemed to shine with the brilliance of a rainbow in the mist.[13]

In the initial apparitions, Mary directed Juan Diego to go to the bishop of Mexico City, the Franciscan Juan de Zumárraga, with the message that she wished for a Catholic Church to be constructed on Tepeyac Hill, the site of these visions. Doing as he was instructed, Juan Diego delivered this message to the bishop but was unsuccessful in obtaining his consent. And who can blame the bishop? Juan Diego's request, in the bishop's mind, was likely chalked up to nothing more than an overactive pious imagination. He told Juan Diego to ask the "Lady" for some sign of authenticity that would corroborate her claim to being the mother of Jesus.

When Juan Diego informed the Lady of the bishop's request on December 12, she complied, telling him to go gather the beautiful Castilian roses that were blooming nearby, miraculous in light of the high elevation and cold winter. Doing as he was told, Juan Diego gathered an armful of the roses into the front of his *tilma*, a long homespun cloak woven from agave plant fiber and used as much for carrying bundles of firewood as for keeping warm. Then he made the tedious trek back down the mountain into the city to see the bishop. Upon being announced, he told the bishop he had seen the Lady again, had delivered the bishop's request for "proof," and had returned bearing that proof.

When Juan Diego opened his arms to allow the roses to spill to the floor at the bishop's feet, everyone in the room was astonished to see the near-photographic image of the Blessed Virgin Mary imprinted in the most vivid colors on his *tilma*. This miraculous image, known ever since as that of Our Lady of Guadalupe, has been venerated as a holy object for nearly five hundred years. Like the Eucharistic miracle of Lanciano, the miraculous *tilma* has been exposed to the elements with no regard for preservation of the image. Centuries of exposure to direct sunlight, humidity, soot from candles, countless pilgrims wanting a fleeting touch of the cloth, and the ravages of flash photography have not faded or damaged this miraculous image.

In 1921, during the depths of the Mexican government's bloody persecution of the Catholic Church,[14] someone even detonated a bomb hidden among the flowers on the altar over which the *tilma* was hanging. The blast shattered the windows in the basilica and destroyed everything within twenty feet of the explosion, including the heavy brass candelabra and the large iron crucifix that stood on the altar. The crucifix, which is on display at the basilica, was blackened and twisted by the force of the blast. It even appears as if the crucifix itself had miraculously bent down to absorb the blast and protect the *tilma*, which was utterly unharmed by the attack.

Many scientific studies have been conducted in an effort to ascertain how exactly the image of Mary was imprinted on the fibers. Was it painted? Was it dyed? Was there a sketch drawn underneath over which the image itself was somehow applied? The results of these tests indicate that though embellishments were added later by artisans, the original image itself was neither painted onto the fabric nor applied in some other way known in the sixteenth century. It's just *there*.[15]

Those first millions of converts to Catholicism became

the vanguard of the Catholic Church in Mexico, a country that for the next five centuries, amid many difficulties and sorrows, has remained steadfastly Catholic, due at least initially to the intercession of the Blessed Virgin Mary under the name Our Lady of Guadalupe. My familial roots on my father's side run deep in the hallowed soil of Catholic Mexico and Spain, lands imbued with a deep reverence for the Blessed Virgin Mary, especially because of her singular role as a heavenly intercessor for God's people here on earth.

## A Narrow Escape

In August 1986, my younger brother, Chris, and I went on a sightseeing trip to Mexico City. Most of my father's side of the family hail from Mexico, so this trip was an exciting opportunity for us to get in touch a bit more with our paternal heritage. While we were in Mexico, Chris and I had fun exploring the ancient Indian pyramid complex of Teotihuacán, an hour's drive northeast from Mexico City, as well as the various must-see sites around the metropolis. It's difficult to adequately describe the vast profusion of historical, cultural, and religious treasures to explore in and immediately around this city.

Wanting to wring a few extra hours out of our final day there, I decided at the very last minute to see if we could change our return ticket for Aeroméxico 498 to a later flight. After stopping at the travel agency to check, I found out that even with such short notice, there *was* space available for the two of us on Aeroméxico 172, departing from Mexico City at 4:00 p.m. and arriving in Tijuana rather than

Los Angeles, which meant a slightly longer drive home but was worth it. I made the switch and thought nothing more about it.

Rather than doing anything "touristy" in a secular sense, Chris and I spent our last Sunday in Mexico City making a pilgrimage to the shrine of Our Lady of Guadalupe, built on exactly the same spot where, nearly five hundred years earlier, the Blessed Virgin Mary appeared to Juan Diego. After going to Mass and confession, we explored the basilica and its environs for several hours. I spent a long time prayerfully contemplating the meaning of the miraculous *tilma*, displayed in all its radiant beauty above the main altar, protected by bulletproof and, presumably, bomb-proof glass.

Before long, it was time to head to the airport to catch our flight home. Chris and I settled into our seats, animatedly reliving the highlights of the trip. A couple of hours later, when we landed in Tijuana and the jet taxied to the terminal, I was surprised to see a throng of television news reporters and cameras milling around our arrival gate. I was even more surprised to see our dad in the crowd, looking very worried, anxiously scanning the deplaning passengers to catch a glimpse of . . . us. The wave of relief that swept over his face was palpable. But we didn't as yet understand why he was so relieved and why he was even there to meet us.

He broke the terrible news that the Aeroméxico flight we had originally been booked on—the one I felt prompted to change at the last minute—had been involved in a midair collision with a small private plane over Cerritos a few hours earlier while on its final approach to LAX. Everyone on both planes, as well as fifteen people on the ground, was killed in the fiery crash. I couldn't help but feel the profound connection between that chance decision to take a later flight and how we spent that extra time: making a pilgrimage to this holy site dedicated to the honor of the Blessed Virgin Mary. Even though some may call these events mere coincidence, I see in them a kind of heavenly synchronicity in which the loving intercession of Our Lady really did safeguard my life that fateful day. While I cannot prove that this is the case, I have had, ever since, a quiet, definite certitude that we were kept safe because of her prayers.

Ultimately, only God Himself can miraculously change the course of human events in ways such as this, but few Christians would dispute the truth that God often makes use of saintly men and women as intercessors, enabling them to avert a catastrophe by their heartfelt prayers: *"The fervent prayer of a righteous person is very powerful"* (James 5:16; NAB). In 2 Corinthians 1:10–11, Saint Paul expands on this truth by saying that God "rescued us from such great danger of death, and he will continue to rescue us; in him we have put our hope [that] he will also rescue us again, *as you help us with prayer,* so that thanks may be given by many on our behalf *for the gift granted us through the prayers of many*" (emphasis added). The Bible says that our fervent prayers are "very powerful," even during this earthly life, with all our imperfections, limitations, and distractions. That must mean, therefore, that the fervent prayers of Mary and the saints in heaven—who Hebrews 12:23 says have been "made *perfect"* in righteousness—must be far more powerful than ours. My narrow escape from the Aeroméxico crash was another important reason for, and confirmation of, my devotion to the Blessed Virgin Mary.

## Jesus Christ: The Second Adam

Many people are not acquainted with the profound maternal love that Mary, the mother of Jesus, has for all who love her Son. But the Bible is clear that she does indeed have this role in the Church. Because she is the mother of Jesus and loves him with all her heart, mind, and strength, and Christians are members of his mystical body, as Saint Paul emphasizes in 1 Corinthians 12, she must love us as well. As Jesus said to those who love and believe in him, "I am the vine, you are the branches" (John 15:5). In the same way that you can't see a vine without also simultaneously seeing the branches on the vine, Mary loves all those who are members of Jesus's body.

The Catholic Church teaches that because, as the Bible says, those who love God and bear testimony to Jesus are also the "offspring," of the Woman, they should venerate her as their mother, in and through Christ. Revelation 12:1–12 speaks of the apostle John's apocalyptic vision of "a woman clothed with the sun, with the moon under her feet, and on her head a crown of twelve stars; she was with child" (a nearly exact description of the image of the Virgin Mary on Juan Diego's *tilma*, as it happens). He describes this woman as the target of "a great red dragon" who seeks to devour the male child she gives birth to (Jesus Christ), yet God protects her and the child. "Then," he says, "the dragon was angry with the woman, and went off to make war on *the rest of her offspring, on those who keep the commandments of God and bear testimony to Jesus*" (Rev. 12:17, emphasis added).

It became for me something like a treasure hunt. The more I began digging into the Catholic Church's Marian doctrines, especially as they are reflected in the Bible and the teachings of the early Christians, the more some startling truths about Mary jumped out at me. In Romans 5:12–14, I read that Adam was a "type" of Christ. The word "type," in a biblical context, refers to someone or something in the Old Testament that prefigured or foreshadowed someone or something greater that would appear later. A key rule of biblical typology is that the Old Covenant type is always inferior, imperfect, and incomplete when contrasted with the person or thing that fulfills it in the New Covenant. In other words, the fulfillment is always superior to the type that foreshadowed it.

Saint Paul's teaching about sin and redemption in Romans 5:12–14 opened my mind up to the fact that Adam prefigured Christ in that from him the whole human race received life. We are the sons and daughters of Adam according to the flesh. Christ is the one who perfectly fulfills the prefigurement that Adam could only imperfectly symbolize and point to. Adam's sin brought death and misery to the human race (see Genesis 3). Christ's sinlessness brought life and peace to those who accept his free gift of salvation. As he himself declared, "For God so loved the world that he gave his only Son, that whoever believes in him should not perish but have eternal life. For God sent the Son into the world, not to condemn the world, but that the world might be saved through him" (John 3:16–17). By his life, death, and Resurrection, Christ undid the damage wrought by Adam. Adam poisoned himself and the rest of the human race by his original sin, losing for himself and the rest of us those astonishing primordial gifts: perfect integrity of the will, an enlightened intellect, freedom from sickness and toil, immortality, and perfect friendship with God. These things were all lost to us through the fall. But when Jesus came to redeem us from the slavery of sin we labored under from the time of Adam to Christ, his death atoned us.

Adam brought about sin and death, but Christ, the second Adam, brought about grace and life. Eve, the first woman, said "yes" to the devil and cooperated with *his* plan, but Mary, the "woman" prophesied in Genesis 3:15, said "yes" to God and cooperated with His plan. Just as Eve is "our first mother," the mother of the human race according to the flesh, the Blessed Virgin Mary, the New Eve, is the mother of all Christians according to the Spirit.

Eve succumbed to the wiles of the Serpent in the garden. She fell for his Big Lie: "You will not die" if you eat of the forbidden fruit of the tree of the knowledge of good and evil. "God knows that when you eat of it your eyes will be opened, and you will be like God, knowing good and evil" (Gen. 3:5). When Eve fell into this original sin, she became quite literally the devil's accomplice. But when God confronts Adam and Eve about their rebellion He offers them hope in the midst of their self-inflicted devastation, saying, "I will put enmity between you and the woman, and between your seed and her seed; he shall bruise your head, and you shall bruise his heel" (Gen. 3:15).

This statement is hugely significant because when God referred to the "woman" who would be an enemy of the devil, He could not have been speaking about Eve, even though she is mentioned again in the very next verse as the "woman" who will henceforth (as is true of all women ever since) experience "pain in childbearing" as one of the maledictions caused by her and Adam's sin. The "woman" here is someone far in the future, the Blessed Virgin Mary, the one who, by her *fiat,* her "yes" to God's plan of salvation through Christ ("Let it be done to me according to your word," Luke 1:38), would bring forth the Messiah and Redeemer, Jesus Christ, who would crush the head of the Serpent.

This leads to another important Catholic Marian doctrine, that Mary was sinless for her entire life, *not because of anything she herself did,* but because God saw fit to bestow on her the singular gift of being sinless. Mary's lifelong sinlessness, which the Catholic Church refers to as her Immaculate Conception, is God's doing from beginning to end. And when Catholics honor and venerate Mary's sinless perfection it in no way takes anything away from God or detracts in some fashion from His infinite goodness. Rather, it recognizes the great blessings He bestowed on her out of love. It is a fulfillment of Mary's own prophecy in Luke 1:48–49 where she said, "Behold, henceforth all generations will call me blessed; for he who is mighty has done great things for me."

As we are told in Genesis 2, God formed the first Adam from dirt—the elements of the immaculate, perfect earth. And Adam himself was created sinless, as was Eve. You might say that in a very literal sense, they were the first "Immaculately Conceived" human beings. Just as God used the immaculate "mother earth," so to speak, to create the first Adam, so, too, He chose an immaculate mother for His Son, Jesus Christ. Mary in her Immaculate Conception is a perfect and superior fulfillment of the "immaculate" earth from which Adam sprang.

Types and their fulfillments abound in the Bible. Moses was a type of Christ. He rescued the Israelites from their bondage to the Egyptians, leading them out of Egypt, down through the Red Sea (miraculously parted for them by God), and into the wilderness of Sinai, where they wandered for forty years before entering into the Promised Land. Jesus rescues us from the bondage and slavery to sin and the devil. Through the sacrament of baptism, he leads us down through the "red sea," which is analogous to being saved by the blood of his cross (see Rom. 6:3–11; 1 Cor. 10:1–5). The saving waters of baptism[16] are the fulfillment of the waters of the Red Sea: by passing through them unharmed, the Israelites were saved.

The paschal lamb mentioned in Exodus 12 was also a type of Christ. It was to be sacrificed and its blood sprinkled on the doorposts and lintels of the Israelites' homes, its flesh cooked and eaten. These things prefigure Christ's death on the cross and how his shed blood protects those who love him from the eternal death caused by sin.[17] The manna from heaven, which miraculously appeared on the ground and fed the starving Israelites as they wandered in the desert before reaching the Promised Land, is a type of the Holy Eucharist, the "bread which came down from heaven," that Jesus speaks of in John 6:32–42. He even specifically connects his doctrine of the Eucharist as being a superior fulfillment of the manna. These few examples of biblical types will help us understand the Marian significance of another striking Old Covenant type: the Ark of the Covenant.

The Ark-Mary connection points toward the Catholic doctrine of the Immaculate Conception, Mary's sinlessness. It was the glorious container that carried the Ten Commandments. In Exodus 25, God directed Moses to construct the Ark out of the most precious materials then available: acacia wood covered with beaten gold. It was to be made as perfect as humanly possible. Why? Because it would carry within itself the Written Word of God. The Ark is a prefigurement of the Blessed Virgin Mary, who, as the Ark of the New Covenant, was chosen by God to carry within her own body the Word of God in Flesh—Jesus Christ.

The parallels between the Old Testament Ark of the Covenant and Mary are numerous and striking. For example, the words of the angel Gabriel to Mary in Luke 1:35— "The Holy Spirit will come upon you, and the power of the Most High will overshadow you; therefore the child to be born will be called holy, the Son of God"—are strongly reminiscent of what we read in Exodus 40:34–35: "Then the cloud covered the meeting tent, and the glory of the

Lord filled the Dwelling. Moses could not enter the meeting tent, because the cloud settled down upon it and the glory of the Lord filled the Dwelling."

In 2 Samuel 6, we read about how, after the Ark had been captured in a battle with the Philistines, King David rallied his troops to recover the Ark and return it to Jerusalem. Several things happen that directly parallel what transpired when the Blessed Virgin Mary went in haste to visit her cousin Elizabeth, who had miraculously conceived a child (John the Baptist) in her old age. First, as the Ark was brought to him, King David leapt with joy (2 Sam. 6:14–16), just as the unborn John the Baptist leapt for joy in his mother's womb when the Blessed Virgin Mary, carrying the Christ child in her womb, came near (Luke 1:41).

Seeing the Ark being borne back in triumph, King David uttered in awe-filled gratitude to God, "How can the ark of the Lord come to me?" (2 Sam. 6:9). Elizabeth said to Mary, "Who am I that the mother of my Lord should come to me?" (Luke 1:43). David commanded that the Ark be sent into the hill country of Judea to visit the household of Obededom the Gittite for three months (2 Sam. 6:10–12); Mary "went in haste" to the hill country of Judea to visit her cousin Elizabeth (Luke 1:39–45, 65). While the Ark was present in Obededom's home, it "blessed [his] household" (a euphemism for a surge in fertility). God blessed Elizabeth and Zechariah with the gift of a child in their old age.

The Ark-Mary imagery appears again in Revelation 11:19 and 12:1–17, where Saint John sees the Ark of the Covenant appear in heaven and immediately afterward he sees Mary, the "woman clothed with the sun."

For me, these and other biblical parallels helped make the case for Mary's sinlessness. Following the countless other typological examples in Scripture, I could not find a convincing and biblically coherent way to argue against the fact that the type is always inferior to its fulfillment.

Who could be more deserving of respect and honor than the woman whom God chose to be the mother of Jesus Christ? As the Bible makes clear, when we honor and glorify God's saints, foremost among them the Blessed Virgin Mary, we are not in any way "detracting" from God Himself any more than praising a beautiful work of art is detracting from the artist who created it. The honor and veneration the Catholic Church shows to Mary pales in comparison to that which God has shown her. As Jesus said about the saints, "The glory which thou hast given me I have given to them" (John 17:22).

# 8

## How 'bout Them Saints?

MYSTICS, MARTYRS, AND MIRACLE-WORKERS

I WAS A KID DURING NASA'S GLORY DAYS OF SPACE exploration in the 1960s and '70s, when the Mercury, Gemini, and Apollo missions were launched. My bedroom was filled with scale-model rockets and space capsules I built and painted, the better to imagine those daring celestial adventures. I remember my dad waking me up around 10:30 on the night of July 21, 1969, so I could join him and my mom in the den to watch—live, on our black-and-white console TV—as Apollo 11's Neil Armstrong became the first human being to set foot on the moon.

"You're witnessing history, son!" my dad enthused as he tousled my hair. (He was every bit as excited as I was.)

Armstrong's "one small step for man, one giant leap for mankind" was electrifying and made an abiding impression on me. Though I spent countless hours with my G.I. Joe action figures reenacting World War II exploits like those I saw on shows like *The Rat Patrol* and *12 O'Clock High*, astronauts ranked even higher than military heroes. Those silver-suited adventurers who thundered heavenward into the deadly unknown of outer space were larger than life and supremely brave—willing to risk everything, even their lives, in pursuit of celestial objectives. I constantly imagined myself doing what they did. Ask any kid back then who his heroes were, and most of them would have mentioned astronauts.

And yet, as might be expected of a kid raised in a devout Catholic family, I knew even then that there were heroes at a level above even that of astronauts. They were the saints: the men, women, and children who loved God so much that they let nothing stop them from seeking Him. My parents had a large family library jammed with books about the saints and their heroic virtue, from Butler's *Lives of the Saints* to individual volumes. When my folks grounded me or sent me to my room, I secretly enjoyed those long hours of uninterrupted reading. I became fascinated with how these ordinary people were transformed by God's grace into extraordinary paragons of love.

The saints' heroism has been tested in the face of grave dangers, persecutions, and *especially* martyrdom. Even as a child, there was something incredibly inspirational about people who loved God so much that they were willing to *die* for Him. While most kids daydreamed about becoming athletes or cowboys, I often imagined myself as a fearless martyr for the faith who, in spite of dungeon, fire, and sword, withstood imaginary torture at the hand of pagan emperors rather than deny Christ.

More than just the stuff of legend, these real people

have shown me that living virtuously is not something reserved for the lucky few. Anyone can become a saint if he or she is willing to accept and cooperate with God's loving grace. While it is true that "the spirit is willing but the flesh is weak," grace builds our weak, selfish, fickle human nature. God's grace works on our fallen human nature like a sculptor works on a hulking block of marble. With each blow of his hammer upon the chisel, a piece that doesn't belong is chipped away and a new hint of the masterpiece is revealed. For most people, even saints, the lifelong process is slow and gradual, difficult, and sometimes painful. Some of the greatest saints were once great sinners. King David, Mary Magdalene, and Augustine of Hippo immediately come to mind. But there are many others, including Callixtus (an embezzler), Pelagia (a promiscuous actress), Moses the Ethiopian (a cutthroat gang member), Alipius (obsessed with blood sports), Mary of Egypt (a seductress), Olga (a mass murderer), Vladimir (a rapist and a murderer), John of God (an out-of-control gambler), Margaret of Cartona (a rich man's mistress), and Matt Talbot (a chronic drunkard).[1] Quite a collection of characters!

Saint Augustine of Hippo (354–430) is perhaps most well known for his wild and crazy lifestyle before his deep conversion to Christ. As he explains in his classic autobiographical work *Confessions,* his youthful energies were focused on pursuing sexual pleasure, excelling as an orator, and cultivating knowledge of arcane philosophy, specifically the Gnostic cult of Manichaeism.[2] Augustine describes his former self as "an abyss of corruption."[3] By his own admission, he had completely sold out to the fourth century's equivalent of sex, drugs, and rock 'n' roll. Eventually, by the time he was thirty years old, Augustine had seen through Manichaeism's empty philosophical pretensions and had begun yearning for the fullness of truth that he knew was the only thing that could truly satisfy him. He began reading the New Testament, which opened his mind and heart to the fact that by faith in and obedience to Jesus Christ he would obtain that truth and happiness he sought, and salvation besides.

Like Augustine, all of these sinners-turned-saints give us living proof that if God can do it for them, He can do it for you—no matter where you've been or what you've done.

The raw material that goes in at the beginning of the assembly line is a fallen human nature, a bundle of unruly passions, selfishness, appetites, and addictions. The miracle of God's grace is that what rolls out the other end is a true masterpiece of love, brighter and shinier than the stars of heaven. Saint Paul, himself once a proud, vengeful, murderous man, explains how and why this improbable transformation takes place:

> For the foolishness of God is wiser than men, and the weakness of God is stronger than men. For consider your call, brethren; not many of you were wise according to worldly standards, not many were powerful, not many were of noble birth; but God chose what is foolish in the world to shame the wise, God chose what is weak in the world to shame the strong, God chose what is low and despised in the world, even things that are not, to bring to nothing things that are, so that no

human being might boast in the presence of God. He is the source of your life in Christ Jesus, whom God made our wisdom, our righteousness and sanctification and redemption. (1 Cor. 1:25–30)

Reflecting on this passage, I realize that I am far from sanctity. I can *see* the coastline of sanctity, hazy in the distance, like a swimmer crossing the dark, deep, freezing waters of the English Channel sees, far off, his shimmering goal, remote yet beckoning. I know that *reaching* it will involve effort and discomfort, and as I dog-paddle my way in that direction, pulled along by the current of God's grace, I'm encouraged by the example of the saints, who give it everything they've got and flat out power their way toward the goal of heaven. They prove to the rest of us that those who are determined to become saints and give it everything they have will make it.

Some succumb to the whispered innuendo "you just don't have what it takes to be a saint, so why bother?" Like the kid who idolizes a famous athlete, admiring his powerful physique and extraordinary speed and accuracy, we can admire the saints for the beauty and strength of their virtue and their ability to do great good for others. But when the kid looks in the mirror and is reminded of how scrawny and weak his arms are, how slow and clumsy he is, it's not hard for him to give in to the temptation to despair of ever becoming strong. The truth is, though, every famous athlete was once a scrawny kid. The difference between them and all the countless wannabe superstars is that the superstars made the effort to achieve their goals.

The beauty of becoming a saint (as the saints themselves tell us) is that it isn't a matter of one's own sheer iron will that makes it happen. God's all-powerful grace transforms the spiritually scrawniest of us into the most beautiful and robust of specimens. As the Bible says, with God "all things are possible." The saints are models for what we all can become, if we would just do what they did and go "all in" for the cause of Christ. I have known men and women who are single-minded (not fanatical), determined (not obsessed), and completely convinced (not brainwashed) that their true and lasting happiness can be found only in God. The saints, once they realize that nothing else can provide the true and lasting happiness we all crave, give up everything to have God.

The more I read the lives of the saints, the more I realized that it was precisely in their *lives* that they learned how to love God above all things. As I got older, it wasn't just martyrs who captured my attention. True, according to Catholic teaching, martyrdom "seals the deal," so to speak,[4] but most saints do not die a martyr's death. Most learn to co-operate with God's grace and become more and more conformed to the likeness of God, the One they love the most in the whole world.

As I mentioned, as a boy I was very taken with Saint Dominic Savio. He was a protégé of another great saint who also fascinated me, the miracle-working priest Don Bosco (1815–1888).[5] Saint Dominic Savio's radiant virtue and fearless courage of conviction, especially when it came to preserving his purity (something, I confess with sadness, I was not successful in doing as a youth), really impressed me. His motto "Death before sin!" was a shining ideal I wanted to emulate though I didn't have his iron will. Even so, I'm quite sure his good example, passed down to me through the books I devoured, played a role in helping me avoid some of the worst moral pitfalls I could have so easily fallen into and into which I saw others around me fall with regularity. Saint Dominic Savio was an ideal for me, someone whose life of unswerving virtue was one I could aspire to, though in many ways I fell far short of it. I saw in him the kind of young man I wanted to be, even if that lofty goal was something I'd never reach. My halting, haphazard, halfhearted attempts to remain pure, helped along by God's grace at every step, were in themselves good things, and I am convinced that God smiled at even those meager efforts.

The story of the heroic Mexican Jesuit Father Miguel Pro, executed by government firing squad in 1927, also made a big impact on me as a kid. Ordained just two years before his death, he received permission to minister undercover in Mexico City to Catholics suffering beneath the recently enacted anti-Catholic laws that made it illegal to celebrate Mass, hear confessions, baptize babies, and in any manner publically profess the Catholic faith.[6] The Mexican authorities hunted him in vain, repeatedly confounded by his last-minute escapes and array of ingenious disguises. Father Pro masqueraded as a chauffeur, a garage mechanic, a street sweeper, a farmworker, and even a dapper, cigar-smoking man-about-town in a straw boater and a flashy suit, enabling him to slip undetected into a situation in which he could clandestinely hear confessions, baptize babies, marry couples, pray with, console, and encourage people, and, most important, celebrate Mass. No danger was too daunting for Father Pro.

Once, he donned a policeman's uniform (how he got hold of one, I'll never know) and brazenly entered Mexico City's central jail, ostensibly to "interrogate" a Catholic prisoner. Leaning against the bars of the cell and pretending to jot down notes, he heard the condemned man's confession and unobtrusively gave him Holy Communion.

Perhaps Father Pro's most audacious tactic was to impersonate an undercover police detective. He once arrived at a safe house where he had planned to secretly celebrate Mass only to find policemen outside surveilling the place. Rather than skedaddle, which would arouse suspicion, he strode right up to the clueless cops, pulled back the lapel of his coat quickly, as if flashing his badge, and informed them that he believed a *priest* was hiding inside the house and he was going inside to search it. Once inside, he stuffed his priestly vestments, Mass kit, and other incriminating items into his satchel and, minutes later, stepped back outside feigning disappointment. "False alarm," he sighed, and then left. He noted wryly in his diary that he "received two superb military salutes from the policemen."

Eventually, though, the police caught up with Father Pro. Framing him for a crime he had no part in or even knowledge of, and without even a show trial, the Mexican president, Plutarco Calles, ordered the priest's summary execution by firing squad to make an example of him. On the morning of November 23, 1927, after forgiving and blessing the riflemen, Father Pro was led from his cell. He knelt in prayer for a few moments and, rising, refused a blindfold and stood calmly in front of a bullet-scarred adobe wall, facing his executioners with arms outstretched. With a rosary in one hand and a small crucifix in the other, he cried out *"Viva Cristo Rey!"* (Long live Christ the King!) as the volley of bullets cut him down.

Calles's order that the execution be filmed and photographed for propaganda purposes was a serious miscalculation. It backfired when the Mexican people's reaction to the graphic pictures was the opposite of what Calles had expected. The streets in Mexico City along the route of Father Pro's funeral procession were thronged with thousands of Mexican Catholics silently protesting his death. They conducted the martyr's body through the streets attired in his priestly cassock and surplice, a capital crime under the anti-Catholic laws at that time. In 1988, Miguel Pro, S.J., was beatified by Pope John Paul II. In his sermon, the pope declared that Father Pro's

life of sacrificing and intrepid apostolate was always inspired by a tireless evangelizing effort. Neither suffering nor serious illness, neither the exhausting ministerial activity, frequently carried out in difficult and dangerous circumstances, could stifle the radiating and contagious joy which he brought to his life for Christ and which nothing could take away (see John 16:22). Indeed, the deepest root of self-sacrificing surrender for the lowly was his passionate love for Jesus

Christ and his ardent desire to be conformed to him, even unto death.[7]

Blessed Miguel Pro was one of the many saints whose lives and heroic examples made a positive impression on me growing up. Luckily for anyone interested in learning more about these amazing people, there are several excellent works that introduce modern readers to their lives and times. Whet your appetite with John J. Delaney's *Dictionary of Saints* (Image Books, 2005) or Brian O'Neel's *39 New Saints You Should Know* (Servant Books, 2010).

I have a theory to explain why the Catholic Church has been such a successful "saint-making" factory, sending forth countless courageous men and women, boys and girls, who loved God with such ardor that nothing could dissuade them from turning away from Him or denying Him—not even the threat of death. The Catholic Church, being the one true Church established by Jesus Christ, has the rich, loamy "soil" in which the roots of the human soul can sink down deep and be cultivated in holiness. These "nutrients" include the Holy Bible; the Apostolic Tradition; the Sacraments, especially the Holy Eucharist; the intercession of the Blessed Virgin Mary and the saints; a highly developed, coherent moral theology and a keen understanding of natural law; twenty centuries of service to the poor and suffering; and a host of other grace-filled additives that can stimulate and nurture the grace of God in the soul. To these positive saint-making ingredients can also be added the Church's two thousand years of accumulated wisdom and experience in the spiritual life, prayer, and self-knowledge. All of these things combine to form that rich and life-giving soil for the soul.

The Catholic Church, through its saints, reminds us that God's grace builds on our weak human nature, with all its frailty and instability, with all our weaknesses and failures. Our lives are filled with failures, and God's grace is the one thing that can work with our defects, heal them, and raise them to become the virtues with which He can make saints out of us. To say it differently, an acorn's purpose is to become an oak tree, just as your purpose and mine is to become a saint. Most times, though, when you fling an acorn into the forest, it doesn't become an oak tree. It doesn't achieve its purpose. Why? Because, left to itself, it almost certainly will not fulfill its potential due to lack of water, soil, and protection. But if the forester carefully plants the acorn far enough down in the right soil, an oak tree may well arise. This, I believe, can account for the fact that the Catholic Church has produced countless saints down through the ages who have not only lived exemplary lives of service and love for others (once they were converted) but also performed astounding miracles—prodigies of physical healings, raising the dead, bilocation, prophesy of future events that came true, and even command over the forces of nature.[8]

And along the way, masterpieces of spiritual theology by Catholic authors have abounded for those who are willing to take them up, learn from them, and be transformed by their wisdom. Saint Francis de Sales's *Introduction to the Devout Life,* a spiritual classic in the Western tradition, explains how to steadily move forward in loving God, especially by understanding the day-to-day ways in which truly loving him is expressed in truly loving (and putting up with!) one's neighbor. I learned a lot from this book about prayer and how to more positively and effectively deal with those contradictions, inconveniences, and setbacks that we all inevitably encounter.

Saint Thérèse of Lisieux's *Story of a Soul* is a window into the secret garden of this extraordinary young woman's interior life. Even if for no other reason than to find some respite and quiet amid daily life's cacophony of interruptions and distractions, you should read this book. It reveals so beautifully that it is the small, simple, and hidden things that God desires from us, not grandiose gestures or hectic programs of activity or ostentatious penances. Partly due to the power of this book, Blessed Pope John Paul II declared Saint Thérèse a Doctor of the Church, because she provides us with, as he put it, "an enlightened witness of faith which, while accepting with trusting love God's merciful condescension and salvation in Christ, reveals the mystery and holiness of the Church."[9]

*The Way of Perfection* and *Interior Castle* by Saint Teresa of Ávila and *Dark Night of the Soul* by her contemporary, Saint John of the Cross, are profound meditations on the stages of spiritual growth, which Teresa likened to seven mansions within the castle. Those who are the weakest in the spiritual life and the most vulnerable to temptations are in the outermost mansion. As one progresses in the virtues and in overcoming sins, moving from the lower stages of conversion into the stages of purification, one eventually arrives at the seventh mansion, which is the soul's mystical union with the Triune God through mental prayer, especially contemplation. John of the Cross brilliantly complements Teresa by elucidating the trials and difficulties souls making spiritual progress tend to go through, especially aridity—the sometimes desolating feeling that God is far away. In that phase of purification, prayer can be difficult and tedious, there are no interior consolations or feelings of God's presence and love, and the soul is tempted to surrender and turn back. But, as Saint John of the Cross explains, this "dark night of the soul" will pass in due time and the shining dawn of experiencing union with the Lord will follow.

The list of works by other Catholic saints that I would recommend includes Saint Augustine's monumental *City of God,* Saint Robert Bellarmine's *The Art of Dying Well,* Thomas à Kempis's *The Imitation of Christ,*[10] Saint Ignatius of Loyola's *Spiritual Exercises,* G. K. Chesterton's *The Everlasting Man,* and the incomparable Fulton J. Sheen's *Life Is Worth Living.*[11] Reading these masterpieces of the spiritual life is, as the old saying goes, like sitting on the shoulders of giants. Not only do the great saints themselves provide us with rich and compelling insights into God's love for us, they also draw upon the wisdom and perception that came from earlier saints. And what they all tell us is really just a variation on a theme: "For God so loved the world that he gave his only Son, that whoever believes in him should not perish but have eternal life. For God sent the Son into the world not to condemn the world, but that the world might be saved through him" (John 3:16–17).

The Bible uses the word "saint" to refer to those members of the Body of Christ who are still in this life, part of the "Church Militant" (Acts 9:13, 32 and 26:10; Phil. 4:21; Eph. 4:12). Not long after the last of the twenty-seven books of the New Testament were composed, the term "saint" (Greek: ἅγιος; Latin: *sanctus*) began to be more closely associated with those members of the Body of Christ who had gone on to glory and now reigned victorious with Christ in heaven. This practice did not imply that referring to saints on earth, the biblical usage, was excluded. In the Catholic Church "sainthood" is not always synonymous with "canonization."

*The Catholic Encyclopedia* points out that "the Catholic Church canonizes or beatifies only those whose lives have been marked by the exercise of heroic virtue, and only after this has been proved by common repute for sanctity and by conclusive arguments." This means that, in addition to provable evidence for a life of heroic virtue, even if that virtue manifested itself later in life, verifiable miracles (not uncommonly a sudden and medically inexplicable healing from a life-threatening disease) must be documented after a rigorous scientific effort to disprove them has been carried out.[12]

When I explain to someone what the Catholic Church means by the doctrine of the Communion of Saints, I've found it's helpful to share four biblical truths in the following order:[13]

The first truth is that **the Church is the Body of Christ.** This is a metaphor that goes way beyond the metaphorical. The Church really is Christ's mystical body insofar as we really do become intimately united with him in such a way that we share an organic unity with everyone else who is united to him. Passages such as Romans 12:4–5 and 1 Corinthians 10:16 and 12:12–27 really drive home this point. In fact, Saint Paul says in Romans 12:4–5: "For as in one body we have many members, and all the members do not have the same function, so we, though many, are one body in Christ, *and individually members one of another* (emphasis added)."[14] He returns to this theme in 1 Corinthians 12:12–13, adding, "For just as the body is one and has many members, and all the members of the body, though many, are one body, so it is with Christ. For by one Spirit we were all baptized into one body—Jews or Greeks, slaves or free—and all were made to drink of one Spirit."

Once that first truth has been established, then I point out that the Bible tells us that **there is only one Body of Christ,** not one body in heaven and another on earth. As Saint Paul says, "But now in Christ Jesus you who once were far off have been brought near in the blood of Christ. For he is our peace, who has made us both one, and has broken down the dividing wall of hostility, by abolishing in his flesh the law of commandments and ordinances, that he might create in himself one new man in place of the two, so making peace, and might reconcile us both to God in one body through the cross, thereby bringing the hostility to an end" (Eph. 2:13–16; see also Gal. 3:27–28). In other words, all those who are in Christ—that is, the branches on the vine that Jesus spoke about (see John 15:1–5)—are members of the one, single Body of Christ.

Next, we consider the Bible's teaching that **death does not separate us from Christ.** In Romans 8:35–39, Saint Paul makes this clear: "Who shall separate us from the love of Christ? Shall tribulation, or distress, or persecution, or famine, or nakedness, or peril, or sword? As it is written, 'For thy sake we are being killed all the day long; we are regarded as sheep to be slaughtered.' No, in all these things we are more than conquerors through him who loved us. For I am sure that neither death, nor life, nor angels, nor principalities, nor things present, nor things to come, nor powers, nor height, nor depth, nor anything else in all creation, will be able to separate us from the love of God in Christ Jesus our Lord."

Notice that, if even *death* cannot separate us from Christ, then neither does death have the power to separate us from the other members of the Body of Christ. This means that the saints in heaven are just as much a part of the Body of Christ as those saints here on earth and, as a result, they are just as intimately connected to us here. This is why Saint Paul, who likens each member of the Body of Christ to a part of a physical body (an eye, an ear, a hand, etc.), emphasized in 1 Corinthians 12:21 that "the eye cannot say to the hand, 'I have no need of you,' nor again the head to the feet, 'I have no need of you.'"

This implication is huge! It points directly to the fact that we in this mortal life *need* those members of the Body who have gone on to be with the Lord and, amazingly, they need us, too (see Heb. 11:39–40).

The fourth and final biblical truth I explain is that **all members of the Body of Christ are bound by the law of charity.** This is perhaps best expressed by Saint Paul's teaching in Galatians 6:2: "Bear one another's burdens, and so you will fulfill the law of Christ" (NAB). As we all know, doing this is easier said than done. G. K. Chesterton once observed that "the Bible tells us to love our neighbors and also to love our enemies, probably, because generally, they are the same people."[15] Scripture's teaching about praying for each other is a standing command.

Nowhere does the Bible even hint that after death the saints in heaven forget about us or lose interest in praying for us. In fact, given that James 5:16 says that "the prayer of a righteous man is very powerful in its effects," we can be certain that the prayers of the Blessed Virgin Mary and the saints in heaven, who are *perfected in righteousness* (see Heb. 12:22–24), are extremely powerful in God's eyes.[16]

In Romans 12:10–13, Saint Paul amplifies this message: "Love one another with mutual affection; anticipate one another in showing honor . . . contribute to the needs of the saints." This involves prayer as much as the physical needs that Christ speaks about in Matthew 25. In fact, Saint Paul exhorts Christians to this kind of prayer for one another: "First of all, then, I urge that supplications, prayers, intercessions, and thanksgivings be made for all men, for kings and all who are in high positions, that we may lead a quiet and peaceable life, godly and respectful in every way. This is good, and it is acceptable in the sight of God our Savior, who desires all men to be saved and to come to the knowledge of the truth" (1 Tim. 2:1–4). This statement immediately precedes his teaching that "there is one God, and there is one mediator between God and men, the man Christ Jesus." The Catholic Church teaches that Christ's unique mediatorship as Messiah, Redeemer, and Savior is something no human person could possibly usurp or be a substitute for.

Human beings do not have it within their natural power to save themselves from sin. This is something only God Himself could do for us, which was accomplished by Christ through the Incarnation (i.e., God taking a human nature): "In the beginning was the Word, and the Word was with God, and the Word was God. . . . And the Word became flesh and dwelt among us" (John 1:1, 14).

Perhaps this timeworn aphorism says it best when it comes to describing what it means for God to make us into saints: "Grace is God giving us what we don't deserve, and mercy is God *not* giving us what we do deserve."

A scientist friend of mine named Steve Feeney told me the following true story. During his "atheist phase," he relished any opportunity to confront and confound Christians with his scientific challenges to God. He once challenged his father-in-law, who was also a scientist but a devout Catholic, with the question: "What can overcome entropy, the irreversible degradation of mechanical energy into thermal energy?"

"Love," his father-in-law answered, stopping him cold. Love. That is perhaps the best explanation I can give for what it is to be a saint. The saints love God so much that they will not only live for Him, they will, if necessary, die for Him.

# 9

# Hello, I Love You

## THE CATHOLIC CHURCH'S GOOD WORKS

✝ THE GOSPELS RECOUNT HOW JESUS TIRELESSLY EN-
couraged, fed, and healed everyone around him as he
preached the Good News of salvation, working countless
miracles, curing the sick, and raising the dead. And yet, in
spite of the life-changing truths he proclaimed and the life-
changing miracles he performed, some stubbornly resisted
him. To them, he said, "The works I do in my Father's name
testify to me. . . . If I do not perform my Father's works, do
not believe me; but if I perform them, even if you do not
believe me, believe the works, so that you may realize [and
understand] that the Father is in me and I am in the Father" (John 10:25, 37–38; NAB).

In a similar way, when Christ's public ministry con-
cluded, the Catholic Church he established followed in his
footsteps, serving everyone, rich and poor alike, but especially the outcasts of society: the impoverished and destitute, refugees, prisoners, unwed mothers, the physically

sick and mentally insane, the demon-possessed, orphans and widows, the homeless, alcoholics, drug addicts, prostitutes, slaves, battered women, handicapped people, and abandoned newborn babies. Along the way, many Catholic saints performed astonishing miracle cures and raised people from the dead. Jesus had foretold that this would happen: "Truly, truly, I say to you, he who believes in me will also do the works that I do; and greater works than these will he do" (John 14:12).

He commanded the apostles, "Whenever you enter a town and they receive you, eat what is set before you; heal the sick in it and say to them, 'The kingdom of God has come near to you'" (Luke 10:8–9).

Since those earliest days, service to the poor has always been front and center in the Catholic Church, a consuming passion to put into practice Jesus's command: "And as you wish that men would do to you, do so to them" (Luke 6:31). This is true at the local level of soup kitchens and homes for unwed mothers, and institutionally through the Church's global relief ministries, such as the Vatican's Pontifical Council Cor Unum ("One Heart" in Latin).[1]

As the apostle James puts it so pointedly, "What does it profit, my brethren, if a man says he has faith but has not works? Can his faith save him? If a brother or sister is poorly clothed and in lack of daily food, and one of you says to them, 'Go in peace. Be warm and filled,' without giving them the things needed for the body, what does it profit? So, faith by itself, if it has no works, is dead" (James 2:14–17).

None of this is to imply that all or even most Catholics

are exemplary in their efforts to feed the hungry and take care of the disadvantaged. Sadly, many are not! In fact, it's true that some Catholics have caused many problems and hurt many people by their selfishness, injustice, and greed. No one can deny that. But it remains that this teaching has always been the shining *ideal* given to the Church by Christ, and one that history demonstrates she has always and everywhere strived to promote and practice, even though many Catholics have fallen short of that ideal. However, we cannot forget the countless other Catholics who have selflessly dedicated their lives to serving those in need.

## Hospitals and Health Care

During the first few centuries of the Church, before the rise of hospitals as we understand them today, medical care was an ad hoc service that Christians took seriously, but they had no coordinated means of offering it on a large scale. So, visiting the sick in their homes, as well as serving the poor and homeless, was a task that had to be undertaken in a very person-specific way. Given the huge numbers of sick and poor people, the apostles recognized the need to establish the ministry of the diaconate, a special order of men whose primary focus would be serving others through "corporal works of mercy" (i.e., feeding the hungry, clothing the naked, and so forth). These deacons, starting with the first seven who are mentioned in Acts 6:5, formed the backbone of the Catholic Church's earliest relief efforts in Jerusalem, and later in Rome and throughout the world.

One of the qualifications for a bishop was to be "hospitable" (1 Tim. 3:2), which meant feeding or even taking into his own home those who needed a place to stay or food to eat. This arrangement was good and helpful but not practical in any extensive way. Once the more or less constant waves of Roman persecutions against Christianity officially ended with the promulgation of the empire's Edict of Toleration in 311, followed in 313 by the emperor Constantine's Edict of Milan, which gave legal recognition to Christianity, the Church was able to engage in charitable good works out in the open and on a much larger scale than had been possible before.

The first hospitals were established by Catholics in the East, shortly after the Edict of Milan. By the mid-300s, they had built large hospitals in Edessa and Caesarea in Cappadocia (modern-day Kayseri, Turkey). By the 500s, the Church had established similar hospitals throughout the Mediterranean Basin, including in Alexandria, Egypt, as well as Rome, Lyons, and modern-day Mérida, Spain. A consistent feature of all these Catholic institutions was free health care for the poor and indigent.

In the Middle Ages, Catholic hospitals and other forms of health care became increasingly connected with the monasteries that blanketed Christendom. This was a very good thing, because it enabled the quality of care to improve under the ministrations of the monks, dedicated men of prayer and poverty and learning whose education and diligence helped improve the logistical aspects of running a hospital.

Today, the global system of Catholic hospitals, clinics, and other medical institutions is something we often take for granted, without even realizing that our modern system of health care itself is, in many ways, based on the Catholic Church's pioneering efforts in this area.[2]

## Orphanages

Caring for widows and orphans is so meritorious that the Bible extols it as "religion that is pure and undefiled before God" (James 1:27). Indeed, the Old Testament is replete with warnings about neglecting them, such as this stern reminder from the Lord: "You shall not afflict any widow or orphan. If you do afflict them, and they cry out to me, I will surely hear their cry" (Exod. 22:22–23).[3]

Taking this message to heart, the early Church dedicated a great deal of money and energy to helping both of these groups. As hospitals began to flourish in Christian lands, so did orphanages. While caring for orphans was practiced in ancient Greece,[4] it was something of a novelty in the culture of pagan Rome of antiquity, where infanticide was not uncommon. Human beings, especially infants and children, the elderly, and handicapped people, were seen as expendable and truly valuable only insofar as they could contribute to society. The most typical method for disposing of unwanted children, especially in the case of infants, was abandoning them, exposed to the elements, until they died. As one can imagine, such brutal callousness horrified the early Christians, galvanizing them to seek after the physical and spiritual welfare of such unfortunate children, and thus the nascent Catholic emphasis on Church-supported orphanages began to grow.

Lactantius, a significant fourth-century Christian apologist, described the Catholic Church's constant and unwavering commitment to doing charitable good works for the destitute, poor, and sick:

> [It is] a great work of justice to protect and defend orphans and widows who are destitute and stand in need of assistance; and therefore that divine law prescribes this to all, since all good judges deem that it belongs to their office to favor them with natural kindness, and to strive to benefit them. But these works are especially ours, since we have received the law, and the words of God Himself giving us instructions. . . . [Pagans] perceive that it is naturally just to protect those who need protection, but they do not perceive why it is so. For God, to whom everlasting mercy belongs, on this account commands that widows and orphans should be defended and cherished. . . . Also to undertake the care and support of the sick, who need someone to assist them, is the part of the greatest kindness, and of great beneficence; and he who shall do this will both gain a living sacrifice to God, and that which he has given to another for a time he will himself receive from God for eternity.[5]

Catholic orphanages were a fixture in medieval society all across Christendom, but a dynamic French priest and champion of orphans and the poor, Vincent de Paul (c. 1580–1660), gave this charitable good work new life, through a more organized and systematic character. The founder of several religious orders of men and women, Vincent de Paul's primary concern was to help people get to heaven, but unless physical necessities, such as food, shelter, and clothing, were available to them, he knew that the message of the gospel would likely never be able to take root in their hearts. To remedy the problem of the vast numbers of helpless poor and sick people throughout Europe in his day, he focused his energies on establishing soup kitchens, food banks, free medical clinics, orphanages, old-age homes, and homeless shelters. In fact, his expertise and great success in organizing these outreach programs for the poor became the gold standard that subsequent religious and even secular institutions sought to emulate. Although Vincent de Paul himself lived an austere lifestyle (simple clothes, simple food, modest accommodations), he raised vast amounts of money that were devoted solely to the feeding and clothing of the poor and all his other charitable works. Public records show that by his death he had established more than four hundred "houses of benevolence" across France and many more across other parts of Europe.[6]

## Ransoming Prisoners

One of the more dramatic examples of his leadership in seeking the physical well-being of others is seen in his daring efforts to ransom the tens of thousands of European men and women abducted by Muslim Turkish raiders and forced into the living hell of slavery:

Carried off from their families by the Turkish corsairs, they were treated as veritable beasts of burden, condemned to frightful labor, without any corporal or spiritual care. Vincent left nothing undone to send them aid; as early as 1645 he sent among them a priest and a brother, who were followed by others. Vincent even had his emissaries invested with the dignity of consul in order that he might work more efficaciously for the slaves. The missionaries sent by Vincent not only conducted religious services for the slaves but also acted as intermediaries with their families and worked to secure freedom for some of them. By the time of Saint Vincent's death, these missionaries had ransomed twelve hundred slaves, spending 1.2 million livres on behalf of the Barbary slaves, while enduring affronts and persecutions of all kinds from the Turks.[7]

Here we see the Catholic spirit of "do whatever it takes to help those in need." The priests whom Vincent de Paul sent to minister to the slaves willingly embraced the rigors of slave life themselves. They didn't just serve the slaves, they lived *with* the slaves, baptizing, hearing confessions, celebrating Mass, instructing them in the Catholic faith, all while laboring beside them in drudgery. Here are a few of the countless examples of this selfless spirit of service: the Jesuit Reducciónes in Paraguay among the Guaraní people (established between 1610 and 1670),[8] the Jesuit missions in North America among the Huron, Mohawk, and Iroquois tribes,[9] the indefatigable work for the impoverished indigenous peoples of Peru carried out by the Dominican lay brother Saint Martin de Porres (1579–1639), and the work of Blessed Mother Teresa of Calcutta (1910–1997) among the poorest of the poor in India's slums.[10] Malcolm Muggeridge's 1969 BBC documentary *Something Beautiful for God* (and the book of the same title) chronicled the life and astonishingly abundant good works for the poor that this diminutive Albanian nun carried out while herself living a life of extreme poverty. She said, "God still loves the world and He sends you and me to be His love and His compassion to the poor."

In response to Mother Teresa's critics (especially the late atheist author Christopher Hitchens), the writer William Doino Jr. offered a point-by-point refutation of charges that she was a fraud who only feigned helping the poor. He points out that "by 2010 . . . there were over five thousand Missionary of Charity sisters, serving in 766 houses in 137 countries, and another 377 active brothers serving in sixty-eight houses in twenty-one countries. The Lay Missionaries of Charity, now over twenty-five years old, are also growing, operating in fifty countries."[11]

## Education

According to Proverbs 18:15, "An intelligent mind acquires knowledge, and the ear of the wise seeks knowledge." Heeding this biblical precept, the Catholic Church led the way in helping people acquire knowledge and wisdom through literacy and study of the sciences. It is no exaggeration to say that the Catholic Church quite literally founded Western civilization's educational patrimony, especially the university system.

Centuries before the onset of the Protestant Reformation in the sixteenth century and the appearance of secular colleges and universities in the West, the Catholic Church had developed an impressive array of such institutions of higher learning in important intellectual centers such as Paris, Bologna, Salerno, Chartres, Rome, Ravenna, and Oxford. The hugely influential role of monks and monasteries in their establishment cannot be exaggerated. The contemporary historian Thomas E. Woods Jr. notes that

> Western Civilization's admiration for the written word and for the classics comes to us from the Catholic Church that preserved both through the barbarian invasions. Although the extent of the practice varied over the centuries, monks were teachers. Saint John Chrysostom tells us that already in his day (c. 347–407) it was customary for people in Antioch to send their sons to be educated by the monks. Saint Benedict instructed the sons of Roman nobles. Saint Boniface established a school in every monastery he founded in Germany, and in England Saint Augustine [of Canterbury] and his monks set up schools wherever they went. Saint Patrick is given credit for encouraging Irish scholarship, and the Irish monasteries would develop into important centers of learning, dispensing instruction to monks and laymen alike.[12]

The monastic contribution to Western civilization is immense. Through it, we derived our modern concept of a well-rounded education in literature, the arts, and the sciences, at the primary, secondary, and college levels. The way in which these disciplines came down to us was through the mediation of the countless Catholics who not only pioneered these sciences early on but systematized the most effective ways of transmitting this knowledge to future students through the aggregation of colleges into a university hub wherein a vast array of knowledge across a spectrum of subjects could be inculcated.

"Although many college students today couldn't locate the Middle Ages on a historical timeline," Woods writes, "they are nevertheless sure that the period was one of ignorance, superstition, and intellectual repression."

Nothing could be further from the truth. During the Middle Ages, one of Western civilization's greatest intellectual contributions to the world was developed: the university system, with its faculties, courses of study, examinations, and degrees, as well as the distinction between undergraduate and graduate study. The Church developed the university system because, according to the historian Lowrie Daly, it was "the only institution in Europe that showed interest in the cultivation and preservation of knowledge."[13]

Few people today seem to be aware of this fact. It seems to me a great irony that the Catholic Church's long and storied history of contributions to the Western intellectual tradition, in all its forms and disciplines, has largely been forgotten. True, the fact that the Catholic Church does a lot of good for a lot of people may not itself be a *reason* to be Catholic, but it does point toward an important and compelling reality about the Catholic Church that many of her critics and enemies might wish to ignore or downplay—which is why I'm playing it up in the pages of this book!

The call to love others, especially by serving them, is at the very heart of Jesus's message. You could say it's the very heart itself, because without the love[14] that is expressed in concrete day-to-day actions of kindness and service, one's faith in God can become ossified, hollow, and brittle, just as it had in the case of the Pharisees, whom Jesus frequently rebuked for their hard-heartedness and stiff-necked refusal to condescend to help the poor in anything other than an ostentatious display of almsgiving that was purely for show. He told his followers,

> Take care not to perform righteous deeds in order that people may see them; otherwise, you will have no recompense from your heavenly Father. When you give alms, do not blow a trumpet before you, as the hypocrites do in the synagogues and in the streets to win the praise of others.
>
> Amen, I say to you, they have received their reward. But when you give alms, do not let your left hand know what your right is doing, so that your almsgiving may be secret. And your Father who sees in secret will repay you. (Matt. 6:1–4; NAB)

This may be why the Catholic Church's works of mercy typically go unnoticed and underappreciated. That's how Jesus wanted it to be, after all—not done for applause, for show, or for gain, not even just to garner the sympathy of unbelievers, but because helping others is the *right thing to do*. We all know that helping others quickly becomes debased and compromised when it is motivated by pride and selfishness. This is why I have always been in awe of the vast array of good works performed by the Catholic Church, quietly and unobtrusively around the world on behalf of the least of Christ's brothers and sisters, including—in fact, *especially*—on behalf of non-Christians.

The award-winning film *Of Gods and Men* depicts the final days of a community of French Trappist monks in Algeria, seven of whom were brutally murdered by an Islamist rebel group during the Algerian civil war. The monks had for years served the local Muslim population, dispensing free food, medicine, and quality health care. When the violence became so bad that they were urged to leave lest they be killed, they decided to remain and continue serving, come what may. On the night of March 26–27, 1996, a band of gunmen invaded the monastery and rounded up the monks, holding them captive for two months before killing them.

During the increasingly chaotic and violent weeks before their martyrdom, the prior, Brother Christian, wrote a moving and courageous farewell letter that was found in the monastery after his death. In it, Brother Christian's statement "in God's face I see yours" is an eloquent analogue to Christ's teaching that "as you did it to one of the least of these my brethren, you did it to me" (Matt. 25:40). Seeing the Lord in our neighbor is the impetus for serving him, and seeing our neighbor in the Lord is a reminder that our service is aimed at bringing him closer to the Lord, to see him happy and fulfilled, in this life and the next. These are the "two sides of the same coin" that the Catholic Church endlessly expends in helping others through charitable good works.

For 365 days a year, the Catholic Church puts its money where its mouth is, or better said, it puts its money where the mouths of the poor and hungry are, and it's done so for two thousand years running.[15] We're talking countless hospitals, orphanages, medical clinics, homes for unwed mothers, vocational schools, food banks, soup kitchens, and all the rest, all around the world, serving everyone, not just Catholics. And the really striking thing is that these admirable works of mercy have been undertaken by Catholics in every generation, going all the way back to the time of the apostles.

Lawrence (d. A.D. 258), one of the martyrs of the early Church, is known for the quip he made to his executioners, who were roasting him on a gridiron: "You can turn me over now, I'm done on this side." He hailed from Spain but journeyed to Rome and there ministered alongside Pope Sixtus II as a deacon for a time, until the persecution of the Church under the emperor Valerian broke out. The pope and several deacons were captured by Roman soldiers while celebrating Mass in one of the catacombs outside of Rome. Pope Sixtus was able to direct Lawrence how to quickly divvy up the material possessions of the Church at Rome so that the local Catholic community would not be totally despoiled of its financial means during the persecution.

Lawrence quickly did this, placing the Roman Church's money and matériel in the care of trusted Catholics who could act as custodians until the next pope decided what should be done. The Roman authorities, realizing that Lawrence had access to the Church's "treasure," insinuated that they would have leniency on him if he would turn it over to them. Bargaining for time, he agreed to return in three days with the Church's treasure. True to his word, on the third day, he met the Roman officials at the appointed place and, when they asked for the goods, he gestured around him toward all the poor and lame and destitute of Rome whom he had intentionally gathered for this occasion. "Here are the riches of the Church!" he proclaimed to the amusement of the onlookers and the fury of the authorities. This is believed to be the reason that he was tortured so horribly as part of his martyrdom.

Saint Lawrence's identification of the poor as the Church's "riches," though nothing new at the time, has been a running theme of solicitude for others ever since. The Catholic Church's commitment to performing charitable good works, even in the face of harassment, persecution, and martyrdom, remains permanent and unchanging. It is a hallmark of the subversive character of sanctity. Becoming holy is by its very nature subversive. It seeks to overthrow the established social order of selfish opportunism, to tear down walls that separate people and build up the health and well-being of those who are seen by society as

not valuable, embarrassing, unpleasant, inconvenient—
people to be kept away, out on the fringes, out of sight, out
of mind.

The Catholic laypeople and religious who are doing
this same kind of charitable work around the world in dis-
tressed, war-torn, and poverty-afflicted communities, bringing the love of Christ to those abandoned by society, are
the unsung heroes and heroines who will never be known
or lauded by the public.

They remain in quiet anonymity, selflessly pouring out
the best years of their lives as a sacrifice for others in the
holy obscurity and unassuming charity for which Jesus
promised, "Truly, I say to you . . . every one who has left
houses or brothers or sisters or father or mother or children or lands, for my name's sake, will receive a hundred-
fold, and inherit eternal life" (Matt. 19:28–29).

# 10

# Ah, the Good Life

## THE AWE, WONDER, AND GOODNESS OF GOD

ONE THING I REALLY LOVE ABOUT THE CATHOLIC Church is how wide-open it is to truth, wherever it may be found, its perennial emphasis on the inextricable relationship between faith and reason. It astounds me how so many people today have bought into exactly the opposite perception of the Catholic Church, that Catholicism is synonymous with *anti*scientific, anti-intellectual ignorance and superstition. Nothing, I discovered, could be further from the truth![1]

The facts of history belie that notion, showing that the Catholic Church has always been on the cutting edge of scientific inquiry and progress. The list of prominent Catholic scientists is long and impressive, and includes such worthies as Albert the Great, Roger Bacon, Blaise Pascal, Galileo Galilei (his troubles with the Catholic Church notwithstanding),[2] Gregor Mendel, Louis Pasteur, Wilhelm Röntgen, Guglielmo Marconi, Georges Lemaître, and, more recently, the Jesuit philosopher-scientist Father Robert J. Spitzer.[3]

Being Catholic entails recognizing to the fullest extent our common human duty to make the greatest use possible of our God-given intellectual gifts in pursuit of discovering the mysteries of the universe around us.

For example, Pope John Paul II lauds science, "the extraordinary advances of which in recent times stir such admiration," in his 1998 encyclical *Fides et Ratio*:

> So far has science come, especially in this century, that its achievements never cease to amaze us. In expressing my admiration and in offering encouragement to these brave pioneers of scientific research, to whom humanity owes so much of its current development, I would urge them to continue their efforts without ever abandoning the *sapiential* horizon within which scientific and technological achievements are wedded to the philosophical and ethical values which are the distinctive and indelible mark of the human person. Scientists are well aware that "the search for truth, even when it concerns a finite reality of the world or of man, is never-ending, but always points beyond to something higher than the immediate object of study, to the questions which give access to Mystery."[4]

The awe and wonder I personally experience when I consider the mind-blowingly complex and staggeringly beautiful natural order makes me even more convinced that God loves me and wants me to be happy. Everything around me in nature, as Saint Paul says in Romans 1:19–20, declares the existence of God and it beckons me to know Him more deeply by understanding more deeply the mysteries of His creation.

Every new scientific discovery that enables us to see further into the universe, to unlock yet another puzzle or resolve a long-standing problem, is evidence that we're on the right track as we use our intellects to reconnoiter reality. And it truly amazes me how, with each new discovery, it seems that a whole new panorama of previously unknown aspects of reality come into view. This continual unfolding of new, previously unconsidered aspects of reality is something that has always fascinated me.

When I studied for my undergraduate degree in philosophy, I became enthralled by my investigation of the beauty and structure and symmetry of reality through my coursework in various fields of rational inquiry, including metaphysics (the exploration of being and what it means to be), epistemology (the study of knowledge and how we come to know things), phenomenology (the study of "human experience and of the ways things present themselves to us in and through such experience"[5]), and logic (the science that evaluates and determines the truthfulness or falseness of arguments and the validity or invalidity of their premises).

My philosophical studies helped open my mind even further to the awe and wonder I had always felt, but now I had many new and powerful rational tools with which to explore reality. This has dovetailed well alongside my lifelong fascination with scientific discovery. I regret that I was not much attracted to the "hard sciences" during high school, preferring instead to study Latin, French, Spanish, and other foreign languages, as well as history and literature. The hard sciences seemed too difficult for me to bother with back then. And how I wish I had been more diligent and attentive to them. But thankfully, as I grew older and began to think more clearly and concentratedly about the cosmos and my lowly place in it, I discovered a newfound appreciation for science that really blossomed apace with my philosophical studies.

The philosopher Robert Sokolowski's melancholy observation is one I find profoundly true and meaningful because it expresses something of the awe and wonder I experience as a Catholic who gazes out upon the mystery of this life and the universe in which we live it:

> Since we live in the paradoxical condition of both having the world and yet being part of it, we know that when we die the world will still go on, since we are only part of the world. But in another sense, the world that is there for me, behind all the things I know, will be extinguished when I am no longer part of it. Such an extinction is part of the loss we suffer when a close friend dies; it is not just that he is no longer there, but the way the world was for him has also been lost for us. The world has lost a way of being given, one that had been built up over a lifetime.[6]

I acknowledge the parts of the world we "lose" when someone dies, but I can't help but also see the way in which we have been steadily gaining more and more of the world as science continues to open new doors of perception into the unimaginable vastness and variety of the material cosmos.

I am grateful to science and scientists not only for all the amenities, medical breakthroughs, and life-improving devices they invent, but also for the way they are always pressing forward, outward, upward, into the truth of the natural order. Yes, I thank God that I live in the era of Advil and air-conditioning, but I can only imagine that, if the return of Christ is far off, the astonishing things science has yet to discover will make Advil and air-conditioning look as paltry as pottery and pencils by comparison. The scientific breakthroughs are simply breathtaking, and I'm so glad to be alive to witness them and wonder at what other secrets of the cosmos will be unveiled before my life on this earth is over.

One day, while I'm drinking my morning coffee, I spot a news headline that catches my attention: "NASA's Hubble Spots 'Cosmic Caterpillar' 6 Trillion Miles Long." Six *trillion*? Not as big as the U.S. national debt, maybe, but that's pretty darn huge.[7]

"The object," NASA.gov explains, "lies 4,500 light-years away in the constellation Cygnus." Impressive, but what does that really mean in terms I can wrap my mind around? Turns out, I have an exceedingly difficult time wrapping my mind around this.

A light-year is the distance light travels in one year moving at 186,000 miles per second (the equivalent of thirty-three round-trips from New York to Los Angeles in one second). But *4,500 light-years*? That's 26,453,814,935,617,850 miles—26.5 *quadrillion* miles away from where I am seated right now. And scientists have devised devices that can see objects that far away, indeed much farther away than that.[8]

What does that kind of distance even mean in human terms? Sure, I can understand New York–to–L.A. distances because I've made the trip many times. I can imagine it. And though I've never made the trip, I can grasp the idea of the distance of the earth to the moon because I can imagine it. How about 93 million miles from the earth to the sun? Not so much. That's pushing the limit of what I can imagine. Twenty-six quadrillion miles? No way. I can't relate to that kind of number. Chances are, you can't, either.

Such cosmic distances are simply awe-inspiring to me. They force me to recognize how small I am in comparison with the vastness of the universe that surrounds me. They also shout to me that God exists—indeed, He *must* exist in order for anything else to exist at all—and that He created all this splendor as a sign of His love. Yes, I know, many people today have great difficulty with that notion. Some scoff and reject it out of hand as too "convenient" an explanation for the cosmos around us, but I don't. The more awe and wonder the marvels of the cosmos evoke in me, as science discloses them, the more certain I am that God exists and that this all has a purpose and a meaning and that He is drawing me toward Him through the awesome beauty of the universe.

Maybe I've long enjoyed singing the nineteenth-century hymn "How Great Thou Art" (*"O Store Gud"*)[9] because I'm part Swedish on my mom's side. I find its message to be powerful, majestic, and self-evidently true:

> *O Lord my God, when I in awesome wonder,*
> *Consider all the worlds thy hands have made;*
> *I see the stars, I hear the rolling thunder,*
> *Thy power throughout the universe displayed.*
> *Then sings my soul, my Savior God, to thee,*
> *How great Thou art, how great Thou art.*

Who *hasn't* experienced such moments? No one, I'm convinced. Even atheists find themselves awestruck by the often startling beauty and truth and goodness we encounter in nature. They reflect God's own beauty, truth, and goodness.

For me, these are all glimpses of Him.

A major reason that my "Golden Summer" was so golden was that I had recently gotten my driver's license. There's nothing like the sense of newfound freedom one experiences when, for the very first time, the DMV clerk hands you that small but all-important piece of plastic that certifies you're good-to-go out on the open road.

My dad, wanting to "incentivize" me to get better grades, made my getting an A in chemistry a prerequisite for getting my license. Smart man, my dad. He knew that with more freedom comes more responsibility and, since his teenage son wasn't particularly diligent in the responsibility department, setting a steep price would motivate me to work hard for the privilege of driving. And I did. Though I typically got poor grades in math and science, I wasn't about to allow the recondite mysteries of chemistry to stand in the way of my freedom.

Getting your driver's license is symbolic of the kind of true freedom we all seek, even though not everyone knows how to find it and, if they do find it, how to live in such a way that this freedom can be expanded and enjoyed to the fullest degree. If you do not know the why, you cannot know the how. If you don't know why you are free, you can't know *how* to be free. We all seek freedom and happiness. By this I don't mean the light emotion of "happiness" that comes and goes, a feeling that depends on our mood and circumstances. True happiness in its fullest and most important sense is not an emotion, it is a condition that is far deeper and more real than our passing emotions. "Joy" is often a synonym for this kind of happiness.

Quoting Pope Paul VI, the Catholic author Dan Lord describes this as "peace and satisfaction in the possession of a known and loved good." To this clear and compact definition, Lord adds,

> This peace and satisfaction—joy—comes in degrees, of course, depending on which of the one-hundred-and-twenty-one zillion possible goods you possess. A man smokes an expensive cigar—a small, simple good—and experiences a small, simple peace and satisfaction, a bantamweight joy. Moving up from there into the

heavyweight division, where the highest possible degree of joy corresponds to the highest of all goods, is goodness himself: God.[10]

This is what I mean by true happiness. And to be truly happy, one must be truly free. But this is where things tend to get confusing and bog down in a disparate array of competing and conflicting opinions about what exactly freedom is.

Freedom of will is an indispensable condition for human beings. This freedom is part of us. It exists at the most fundamental level of each person, regardless of his or her circumstances (i.e., it is as true of every prisoner in every jail as it is of every man and woman who comes and goes freely from place to place), in that each of us is free to act according to his or her conscience. Those who exercise their freedom become ever more free. They are free to enjoy the truly good things in life that those who are too busy pursuing sinful things cannot enjoy: peace, contentment, a tranquil conscience, integrity, true love from and for others, and the knowledge that they are headed up the sometimes arduous path that leads to eternal life. That is the true freedom we all instinctively want. It allows us to choose freely and effortlessly to know the truth and do the good. And between the two ends of the spectrum—the "red zone" of freely choosing sin and rebellion and the "golden zone" of virtue and goodness freely chosen—lies the bleak, arid no-man's-land of the "freedom of indifference," where the will hovers above "yes" to God and "no" to

God, never committing to choosing one or the other. Jesus warned everyone who malingers in that insipid quagmire:

> I know your works: you are neither cold nor hot. Would that you were cold or hot! So, because you are lukewarm, and neither cold nor hot, I will spew you out of my mouth. For you say, I am rich, I have prospered, and I need nothing; not knowing that you are wretched, pitiable, poor, blind, and naked. Therefore I counsel you to buy from me gold refined by fire, that you may be rich, and white garments to clothe you and to keep the shame of your nakedness from being seen, and salve to anoint your eyes, that you may see. Those whom I love, I reprove and chasten; so be zealous and repent. (Rev. 3:15–19)

Another big part of my answer to the question *Why be Catholic?* is: "Because the Catholic Church teaches people how to be truly happy." This isn't to say that every Catholic *is* truly happy. Not by a long shot. It's kind of like the question "Why go to college?" Answer: "Because at college they will teach you how to think." But that doesn't mean that everyone who goes to college graduates any better off in the thinking department than they were when they started. The point is, if you apply yourself and work at it, if you listen to the professors and learn from them, then going to college will help you think more clearly and more carefully. It's no big mystery. And the fact that there are many college graduates who don't think carefully and clearly is not an indictment of a college education, nor does it obviate the truth of the statement "Go to college because there you will learn how to think."

In the same way, the fact that there are countless Catholics who live unhappy, even miserable lives does not alter the fact that the Catholic Church really does teach people how to be truly happy. If only they would listen! The problem is, like many college students, many Catholics ignore the Church's teaching and, as a result, never enjoy the benefits that come from living according to those teachings. And here, specifically, I'm referring to the Catholic Church's moral teachings, including those on sexual issues. Catholic teaching on the meaning of good and evil, categories that are manifested in human acts (i.e., "acts that are freely chosen in consequence of a judgment of conscience, can be morally evaluated. They are either good or evil"[11]), is quite often misunderstood and rejected as being "antiquated" or "out of touch" with the modern world and its unique set of challenges or, worse yet, it is met with overt hostility from those who regard Catholic moral principles to be inherently "evil" and thus deserving only of fierce opposition. Examples of this aggressively hostile posture abound among many in the militant "pro-choice" movement.

One journalist recently referred to those who demand that the pope abandon Catholic moral principles on issues such as birth control, homosexuality, and abortion so as to "fix the Church's image and detoxify Catholicism's global brand." Ha. As if the pope were merely a "brand manager." He is not. Nor is the Catholic Church a brand, at least not in the sense that marketers and merchants use the term.

Even so, it is possible to draw some insights from using the brand analogy. It is true that the Catholic Church seeks to improve its "market share" by reaching (and, by God's grace, converting) as many people as possible with the Gospel of Jesus Christ. This is not a new strategy. Here's the original "mission statement"[12] given by Christ two thousand years ago to the leaders of his newly established Church:

> All authority in heaven and on earth has been given to me. Go therefore and make disciples of all nations, baptizing them in the name of the Father and of the Son and of the Holy Spirit, teaching them to observe all that I have commanded you; and lo, I am with you always, to the close of the age. (Matt. 28:18–20)

The Catholic Church seeks to build "customer loyalty" by ensuring that all Catholics come to know and love the Triune God who reveals Himself most fully in Jesus Christ (Heb. 1:1–4). Some would say that this might be true in theory but not in practice. Fair enough. I freely admit that many Catholics have not yet experienced at the heart level what Evangelical Protestants talk about as "being born again." From a strictly biblical standpoint, when Jesus declared to a good and sympathetic member of the Jewish Sanhedrin, Nicodemus, "Truly, truly, I say to you, unless one is born anew, he cannot see the kingdom of God" (John 3:3), he was speaking about the sacrament of baptism and its regenerative effects.[13] But it is also true that the experience people describe as being "born again" and inwardly transformed by God's grace really does require an act of the will, an act of faith in Christ, for as Saint Paul reminds us, "For by grace you have been saved through faith; and this is not your own doing, it is the gift of God—not because of works, lest any man should boast" (Eph. 2:8–9). We are saved by *grace alone* through faith. But God does not have faith in Himself for us. He doesn't "believe in Himself" and then pretend that it was I who believed. No. The believer must have faith. Both God's grace and our ability to have faith in His promises are, as Saint Paul reminds us, *gifts* for which we cannot take any credit. But they are gifts that God means for us to make use of. And this is the starting point for living the Good Life.

God gives us His grace precisely so that we can struggle successfully against our vices and weaknesses, so that we can cultivate virtue, and so that we can grow in our love for the truth. The more we love what is true, the more we will strive to do what is good, for the ultimate Truth and Good are one and the same Person, God Himself.

In Catholic teaching, living the Good Life is, at its very essence, seeking God, choosing God, and loving God. Each human act that is ordered in the direction of the true and the good is ordered toward God, our final end. The great saints have shown us that a life well lived may not be an easy one, but it is joy filled and replete with true happiness because it is a life built on the foundation of what is true and good.

By way of contrast, just look around at those folks whose lives are built on the rickety foundation of fame, fortune, unrestrained sexual pleasure, endless entertainment, and unrestrained indulgence of sensual appetites for food and drink. Do they seem truly *happy* to you? You can see them plastered across the covers of the tabloid newspapers and magazines that blight grocery store checkout counters everywhere. Rich? Yes. Physically beautiful? Sure, at least for the time being, before their glamorous good looks begin to fade, as inevitably happens to everyone (even those of us who were not blessed with glamorous good looks). But it hardly needs to be said that many of these people are deeply unhappy. They ache. They live in the past. They long for the applause and ratings and perks and the strobe-flashing, red-carpet high of the paparazzo's attention. No matter what they make use of to satisfy their constant craving for happiness, everything eventually falls short, leaving them empty, miserable, and unsatisfied. This is true of all human beings. Saint Augustine's famous dictum expresses well the human longing for the infinite goodness who alone can satisfy us: "You have made us for yourself, oh Lord, and our hearts are restless until they rest in you."[14]

But none of these objectives are ever met when Catholic teaching is compromised, watered down, and adjusted to keep up with the times. One particularly telling indicator that this is true is the number of priestly vocations. They go down, even way down, when the truths of the gospel, some of which are hard, are concealed and muffled in ambiguity or, worse yet, outright denied in favor of some faddish trendy opinion. And this is not just my opinion. There's hard, statistical data to back up this claim.

In August 2009, Georgetown University's Center for

Applied Research in the Apostolate (CARA) released "Recent Vocations to Religious Life: A Report for the National Religious Vocation Conference," an exhaustive study of trends in priestly and religious vocations among Catholic men and women. First, to put these results into perspective, note that the Catholic population of the United States increased 61 percent between 1965 and 2012, rising from 48.5 million to 78.2 million.[15]

Other CARA statistics[16] reveal that while the overall number of Catholic priests in the United States, both diocesan and religious, declined precipitously from 58,632 in 1965 to 38,964 in 2012 (a 36 percent decrease) and, even more startling, the overall number of religious sisters (nuns) fell from 179,954 in 1965 to just 54,018 in 2012. That represents a jaw-dropping *70 percent* drop.[17] But here's my point: CARA's "Vocations Report" shows a steep *increase* in vocations to religious orders in which the Catholic faith is proclaimed and lived out uncompromisingly and without ambiguity, even though these orders are still in the minority when compared with the overall number of orders in the United States. Those orders that have compromised their commitment to the Catholic Church's moral teachings (among other aspects of Catholicism) are experiencing an unstoppable free fall in numbers and virtually zero new applicants, whereas more traditional and unabashedly Catholic religious communities, such as the Dominican Sisters of Saint Cecilia (aka the Nashville Dominicans), have for decades experienced a steady increase in vocations among young women.

The Nashville Dominicans' vocation director "reported

that her order has seen a surge in vocations since 1988. In the past 10 years the order has grown by 110 sisters, with 12 to 15 women entering each year. The median age is 36, and the congregation now has 250 members. Twenty-three postulants are expected to enter in the fall, something sister calls a 'gift' for their jubilee."[18] Similarly dramatic increases of membership are happening in more traditionally Catholic men's religious orders, such as the Province of Saint Joseph of the Order of Preachers (Dominican Fathers), headquartered in Washington, DC; the Norbertine Fathers of Saint Michael's Abbey in Southern California; and the Franciscan Friars of the Renewal (both its men's and women's branches), headquartered in the Bronx, New York.

The one thing these different orders have in common is that each has made an intentional choice to affirm and assent to authentic Catholic teaching, to live according to it, and to seek out candidates who are also willing to do these things. These orders thrive. Those that abandon Catholic teaching die. It's simple: paint or get off the ladder. The numbers bear this out.

The situation in Catholic parishes around the country also bears this out: those parishes in which the Catholic faith is preached and taught from the pulpit, where the liturgical life is strong, where practices such as Eucharistic adoration and community outreach to the poor and disadvantaged are central to parish life experience a significant increase in priestly and religious vocations. For example, Saint Patrick's Parish in the Diocese of Columbus, Ohio, is well known for being a "vocations factory," sending young men and women not just to religious orders but to diocesan seminaries. Like similar, more traditional parishes, it is bursting at the seams with many large, young families. The Dominican Fathers who have run Saint Patrick's since its establishment in 1855 are lively, welcoming, caring, and eminently pastoral men. The constant long lines for the confessional are one of the telling features of their parochial ministry, as the sacrament of confession is offered *daily* before and after each of the three weekday Masses, as well as for hours on Saturday afternoon, and before and after each of the four Sunday Masses.

Believe me, when the pastor of a parish goes "all in" and makes the sacrament of confession so readily available, people literally come out of the woodwork and flock to that parish. True story. This is something I have witnessed many times over the last twenty-seven years when visiting similar Catholic parishes around the country, including powerhouses such as Our Lady of Peace Parish in Santa Clara, California; Saint Theresa's Parish in Sugar Land, Texas; and Saint Patrick's Parish in Columbus, Ohio. People gravitate to Catholic parishes that preach Christ and the Catholic faith in their fullness and without compromise. To paraphrase the line from *Field of Dreams*, "If you build it, they will come."

Catholic moral teaching is for many an object of derision, something to be scorned as "medieval." The scorn and derision are not the result of careful examination and thoughtful consideration of the teachings themselves, but are simply a reflexive rejection of anything that might remind us that we are not unbridled pleasure centers who have a natural right to enjoy whatever sensual gratification, however we can get it, from whomever (or whatever) we can get it, for as long as we can get it. We live, after all, in a Viagra-fueled culture that reminds us incessantly that we are all entitled to nearly unlimited pleasure, "safe sex," free contraception, and all the rest of today's secular culture dictates.

My thesis is that when one understands the underlying reasons for these teachings and that they really come from God, rather than from a bunch of celibate old white guys (a common view these days), it becomes so much easier to embrace them and live according to their coherent logic. This logic can be summarized as "know the true and do the good." When it becomes clear to someone that these teachings are true and that assenting to them produces good results, conversions occur. I've seen it myself many times.

The issue of contraception provides a good example of what I mean. The Catholic Church teaches that children are a blessing from God, not a burden or an affliction to be avoided at all costs—a mind-set that is rampant in modern society. The Catholic Church declares:

> Children are the supreme gift of marriage and contribute greatly to the good of the parents themselves. God himself said: "It is not good that man should be alone," and "from the beginning [he] made them male and female"; wishing to associate them in a special way in his own creative work, God blessed man and woman with the words: "Be fruitful and multiply." Hence, true

married love and the whole structure of family life which results from it, without diminishment of the other ends of marriage, are directed to disposing the spouses to cooperate valiantly with the love of the Creator and Savior, who through them will increase and enrich his family from day to day.[19]

Taking the polar opposite view, modern secular society argues that the conception of "unwanted" children is a real danger to be combated. According to Alan Guttmacher, M.D., the former medical director of Planned Parenthood Federation of America, "The pill, in my opinion and that of my colleagues, is an important prophylaxis, perhaps the most important, against one of the gravest sociomedical illnesses extant. That, of course, is unwanted pregnancy."[20]

Dr. Janet E. Smith, a Catholic professor of moral theology at Sacred Heart Major Seminary in Detroit, sums up the situation thusly, highlighting some of the deleterious repercussions of the misguided "too many people" mentality:

We now live in a culture in which we no longer know whether babies are blessings or burdens. The population control people are adamant that there are too many children in this world. They point at a pregnant woman in the Third World and say, "That is the problem; they will consume all of the world's resources. We need to deal with them before it is too late." On the other hand, the pro-freedom people say, "Those are future problem-solvers, they can produce more than they can consume. We need to help them reach their full potential before it's too late."

Up until 9/11, when the World Trade Towers went down, people believed the worst problem there is in the world is overpopulation. Your children are being taught from kindergarten through college that there are simply too many people on the face of the earth. Every child that is being born is being treated as though it's a little environmental hazard, someone who's going to "take a bite of my piece of the pie." Some children think that they are one of those too many people on the face of the earth. I read about one little girl, nine years old, who came home and threw out all of her dolls. Her mother asked her: "Why are you doing that?" She replied: "Because there are too many people on the face of the earth. I'm never going to be a mother." She got the message: she's been taught that it is irresponsible to have children.[21]

To talk about what it means to live the "Good Life" necessarily requires an examination of what is good.

Many people confuse freedom with a kind of "carte blanche" ability to do whatever one wants. In fact, twenty-first-century America is a society steeped in carte blanche mentality, one in which people are encouraged, subtly and not so subtly, to indulge their every desire, no matter how debauched and nefarious, especially in the realm of sex and entertainment. The gradual legalization of practically all forms of pornography in the mid–twentieth century,[22] for example, was one of the harbingers of a radical transformation of American culture from a society predicated on several key presuppositions about what the Declaration of Independence calls "life, liberty, and the pursuit of happiness" into one that has become increasingly mired in moral relativism and an insatiable craving for entertainment, even of the most debased sort.

More than anything else, God wants us to be truly happy. And this is because He loves us. As the old saying goes, "God loves me just the way I am."

Yes, *but He loves you too much to let you stay that way.* That's why He gave us the moral law: it's a guide to the Good Life, the happy life, a life that is focused on knowing the truth and doing what is good.

It is in this light, I believe, that Catholic teaching on moral issues should be understood. Prohibitions against certain immoral behaviors are intended to protect us from the damage those behaviors inevitably result in, both spiritual and physical.

Consider another popular saying: "Friends don't let friends drive drunk." Why not? Because if you're truly someone's friend, if you really care about her health and well-being, you'll step in when necessary to help her avoid a potential catastrophe, right? The great saints all came to understand this about God and about the Church. When they realize that God is looking at them intently, His gaze overflowing with love, it melts their hearts (sometimes only gradually), and they respond with love, understanding that His moral precepts are given out of love, not caprice, out of His burning desire to heal and renew and perfect all that is damaged, weak, and imperfect in us. "Deep calls to deep" (Ps. 42:7).

The French novelist Victor Hugo gives us an apt description of what happens between the human heart and God's love when we cross beyond the threshold of doubt and begin trusting that He wants only what is best for us:

> The power of a glance has been so much abused in love stories, that it has come to be disbelieved in. Few people dare now to say that two beings have fallen in love because they have looked at each other. Yet it is in this way that love begins, and in this way only.[23]

Once we perceive that by living according to God's moral law we can more perfectly and freely respond to His love with love, then the "Thou Shalts" and "Thou Shalt Nots" cease to be arbitrary admonitions from a grumpy God who just doesn't want people to have fun. It's no fun being miserable.

## Longing

Everyone experiences the emotion of longing. We all desire people or things we do not have. A teenage girl longs for the day she can get her driver's license. A salesman longs to make that "big sale" that will bring him a hefty commission. A grandmother longs to see her grandchildren who live far away. A boy longs for acceptance from his classmates and freedom from being bullied at school. A sailor on deployment longs to be home with his wife and children. Loneliness is a very common form of longing. That boundless longing you feel for someone you love can be contained in three small words: "I miss you."

The more intense our longing, the more painful it is. The man who longs for the love and companionship of a woman he can never have, for physical and emotional intimacy with her that he knows he will never experience, is a man in great pain. He desires her ardently, yet she remains inaccessible, out of reach, the impossible dream. Perhaps she is already married to someone else. Or she is much younger than he is. Or, worse yet, she simply may not love him. As songwriters from time immemorial have known, the pain caused by unrequited love is perhaps the worst pain of all.

Sting's beautiful dirge "Mad About You" gives voice to the deep and abiding human longing for love. "I'm lost without you. I'm lost without you!" he cries out, pining for a woman he loves but cannot have. He is in agony. "Tell me, how much longer? How much longer?"

Consider the kind of powerful yet vague sense of longing we all experience at times for . . . *something* . . . we just don't know what. For some, it can be a glorious sunset or majestic mountain vista or the vast, velvet splendor of a diamond-strewn night sky. For me, it can take the form of a beautiful melancholy ache that stirs my soul when I contemplate the haunting grandeur of songs such as Joaquín Rodrigo's *Concierto de Aranjuez* or Maurice Ravel's *Pavane for a Dead Princess*. We all at times experience a longing for something vague and indefinable, something out of reach that we can't quite identify.

This, I believe, is the soul's instinctive yearning for God, as "deep calls to deep" (Psalm 42:8), seeking the one who alone can fully satisfy all our deepest hopes and desires.

> As the deer longs for streams of water, so my soul longs for you, O God. My soul thirsts for God, the living God. When can I enter and see the face of God? (Psalm 42:2–3)

God created each of us for himself, out of love, and he wants only for us to love him in return. This is the joy of the blessed in heaven: They possess, fully and forever, the One who loves them beyond all measure for, as St. John said, "God is love" (1 John 4:8). The magnificent paradox of the human heart is that, though it is itself finite and limited, it has an unlimited capacity for an infinite God.

No one can be truly happy without God, which is precisely the misery of hell. Those who send themselves to hell will spend eternity yearning for God but never having him and never having any hope of ever having him. Theirs is a "constant craving" that will never be satisfied, because they insisted on "my will be done" rather than "thy will be done." And, in the end, because God respects human free will, he allows those who reject him to go their own way, stranding themselves forever in a desolate, self-imposed exile from all that is good. Could anything be more ghastly?

By contrast, the joy of the blessed in heaven is nothing less than the unimaginable, unmitigated bliss that comes from God, for they "shall see him as he is" (1 John 3:2). In heaven, all one's longings, desires, and hopes are utterly, irrevocably, and eternally satisfied by God himself.

As the Bible says, "No eye has seen, nor ear heard, nor the heart of man conceived, what God has prepared for those who love him" (1 Cor. 2:9).

As someone once said, God loves you and there is nothing you can do about it. He wants only to bless you with joy, peace, goodness, faith, hope, and charity and—in other words, true, lasting, real happiness. And isn't that exactly what you long for most?

The crucifix is a reminder of the lengths to which God will go to give these gifts to all who love him.

Let's return for a moment to the driver's license analogy. To be *free* to drive requires learning and living by a lot of rules. If you submit to these rules you have the open road ahead of you, the road to happiness and adventure. But if you refuse to learn and follow those rules, you will get speeding tickets and fines, you will have accidents, you will cause damage to yourself and others, and you may even die. Everyone knows this. God wants us to steer clear of all things that can hurt us.

The world is insistent that this or that activity is perfectly harmless, as long as it's legal and takes place between consenting adults, and no one should tell anyone else that what he or she is doing is "wrong."

"Who are *you* to tell me this is wrong?" they will demand. "Keep your morality to yourself."

Look closely and you'll see a lot of misery among many of the fabulously wealthy, beautiful people who enjoy fame and practically unlimited opportunities for pleasure. I read an article a while ago about a "poorly paid" actor (by Hollywood standards) who got fired from his recurring role on a sitcom. His contract paid him $100,000 an episode! By way of comparison, the main actors on the television show *Friends* were making a *million dollars* an episode. Think about that for a moment. I mean, $1 million an episode is basically Monopoly money to most of us. I personally can't imagine what that would be like. Nor could I imagine pulling down one-tenth that much, $100,000 an episode. And the actor who was making a hundred grand an episode was let go because he complained about not making enough money! What's wrong with this picture?

Money can make life easier, yes, but it can't buy true happiness and lasting contentment. As that great Beatles song says, "Money can't buy me love." I have no idea whether real-estate and media moguls like Donald Trump and Rupert Murdoch are truly happy, deep down inside. But people who sit astride *billions* of dollars in wealth and enjoy every possible convenience and comfort—*especially* such people, it seems to me—appear to be relentlessly restless, even frenzied in their efforts to attain and amass ever more wealth, more holdings, more power. And where does it get them? In the end, none of it goes with them when they die. Jesus talked about this:

> The land of a rich man brought forth plentifully; and he thought to himself, "What shall I do, for I have nowhere to store my crops?" And he said, "I will do this: I will pull down my barns, and build larger ones; and there I will store all my grain and my goods. And I will say to my soul, Soul, you have ample goods laid up for many years; take your ease, eat, drink, be merry." But

> God said to him, "Fool! This night your soul is required
> of you; and the things you have prepared, whose will
> they be?" So is he who lays up treasure for himself, and
> is not rich toward God. (Luke 12:16–21)

Living the Good Life does not involve piling up as much cash and toys as you can get. It isn't about enjoying as much sex as you can possibly enjoy with as many people as you can possibly enjoy it with. It's not about what kind of house you live in or the car you drive. It has nothing to do with your net worth or your position of influence or how many people follow you on Twitter or have friended you on Facebook (or, for authors, how many books you've written). In the end, none of those things will matter a whit, either to you or to God. In the end, not only will you leave it all behind, to others, but you will take nothing with you into the next life except for two things: your love and your sins. And it is on these two things alone that you will be judged.

Yes, there's a lot of misery out there among people who "have it all" or who are busily pursuing that goal. Sure, money buys them a lot of nice things, but money can't make them happy. And worse, the insatiable love of money drags many down into deep unhappiness in this life and, if not overcome by turning to God, into the abyss of the eternal misery of hell, where "their worm does not die, and the fire is not quenched" (Mark 9:48).

So how can we avoid all that? Here is Jesus's answer:

> Do not lay up for yourselves treasures on earth, where
> moth and rust consume and where thieves break in

and steal, but lay up for yourselves treasures in heaven, where neither moth nor rust consumes and where thieves do not break in and steal. For where your treasure is, there will your heart be also. (Matt. 6:19–21)

Jesus also said, "You will know the truth, and the truth will set you free" (John 8:32; NAB). It's simple, really, if not easy. If you live your life focused on knowing what is true and doing what is good, you will be happy, both in this life and in the eternal life to come.

You are free to choose either path, and God respects your freedom. He won't force you to be good. Once you understand that your freedom enables you to be who God created you to be, you can really start down the path of happiness in earnest. When we heed the Church, we heed the truth of Christ proclaimed to us in the Church. Jesus told his apostles, "He who listens to you listens to me, and he who rejects you rejects me" (Luke 10:16). The world offers lies and half-truths. As someone once quipped, "Beware of half-truths. You might get the wrong half."

Consider the analogy of a train. Trains are made to go on tracks, two parallel, confining, rigid steel tracks, which can be thought of as analogous to God's moral laws. A train on tracks is confined and only able to go in the particular direction the tracks will take it. But isn't that exactly what trains are built to do? Trains don't make any sense or serve any productive purpose when they are not on tracks, ready to roll, right? Plop a train down in the middle of a field or on an interstate highway and that train ain't goin' anywhere. It can't, because it was made to run on tracks.

In the same way, human beings who live according to the true and the good are free to do what human beings have been created to do, and that is to be happy. Being on the tracks is analogous to living in accordance with God's will for you, and being on a road or in a cornfield is analogous to rejecting God's will and choosing sin, which always leads nowhere. And worse, it always brings anguish and suffering. (If you don't believe me, take a good long look at the before-and-after pictures of meth addicts posted on the Internet.)

There's another way for you to test this hypothesis. Think for a moment about things you have done in your past that cause you remorse and guilt. Your memories of those misdeeds still stick in your mind like thorns, don't they? It hurts when you think about them, which is why you (like most of us) do your best not to think about your past sins. They bother you because they involve pain. This is your conscience speaking to you. The conscience is that part of the soul that warns us away from things that are bad for us. It is the Klaxon that sounds when your intellect recognizes the spiritual danger you're headed toward, like the *Titanic* heading toward the iceberg. Saint Paul says that "what the law [of God] requires is written on their hearts, while their conscience also bears witness and their conflicting thoughts accuse or perhaps excuse them" (Rom. 2:15). In just the same way that the nerve endings in your hand cause you pain when you touch a hot stove, causing you to pull back before you burn yourself more badly, the conscience is that built-in, hardwired moral GPS system inside your soul telling you to avoid things you know deep down are wrong and bad for you and to do those things you know are right and good for you. Once again, know the true and do the good.

Plain and simple, sin is a rejection of love, God's unrequited love. It is fear based. We fear losing some small good that cannot make us truly happy.

Sin means saying "no" to God's great invitation to love, life, and happiness. Virtue, on the other hand, is the only good response to His love. We should respond with love or, as Saint John says, "There is no fear in love, but perfect love casts out fear. For fear has to do with punishment, and he who fears is not perfected in love" (1 John 4:18).

As C. S. Lewis said, "The Christian does not think God will love us because we are good, but that God will *make* us good because He loves us." His powerful vignette in *The Great Divorce* features a shabby man with a red lizard of lust perched on his shoulder and an angel who offers to remove it for him. It is a profoundly accurate insight into how God loves us just the way we are but loves us too much to let us stay that way.

"Would you like me to make him quiet?" said the flaming Spirit—an angel, as I now understood.

"Of course I would," said the Ghost.

"Then I will kill him," said the Angel, taking a step forward.

"Oh—ah—look out! You're burning me. Keep away," said the Ghost, retreating.

"Don't you want him killed?"

"You didn't say anything about killing him at first.

I hardly meant to bother you with anything so drastic as that."

"It's the only way," said the Angel, whose burning hands were now very close to the lizard. "Shall I kill it?"

"Well, that's a further question. I'm quite open to consider it, but it's a new point, isn't it? I mean, for the moment I was only thinking about silencing it because up here—well, it's so damned embarrassing."

"May I kill it?"

"Well, there's time to discuss that later."

"There is no time. May I kill it?"

"Please, I never meant to be such a nuisance. Please—really—don't bother. Look! It's gone to sleep of its own accord. I'm sure it'll be all right now. Thanks ever so much."

"May I kill it?"

And on it goes until, weary from making excuses and sick at heart over the misery of isolation and shame that his lust has caused him, he gives in and cries out,

"I know it will kill me."

"It won't. But supposing it did?"

"You're right. It would be better to be dead than to live with this creature."

"Then I may?"

"Damn and blast you! Go on can't you? Get it over. Do what you like," bellowed the Ghost: but ended, whimpering, "God help me. God help me."

Next moment the Ghost gave a scream of agony

such as I never heard on Earth. The Burning One closed his crimson grip on the reptile: twisted it, while it bit and writhed, and then flung it, broken backed, on the turf.

"Ow! That's done for me," gasped the Ghost, reeling backwards.

But instead of dying, instead of being unhappy now that lust has been removed, he is transformed into a truly god-like man, tall, strong, and handsome. The lizard, too, is transformed. Once lust is slain, it is reborn as a majestic stallion on whom the man rides off

like a shooting star far off on the green plain, and soon among the foothills of the mountains. Then, still like a star, I saw them winding up, scaling what seemed impossible steeps, and quicker every moment, till near the dim brow of the landscape, so high that I must strain my neck to see them, they vanished, bright themselves, into the rose-brightness of that everlasting morning.[24]

Oh, how I want that for myself. I want God to heal me of all the lusts, anger, fear, pride, and selfishness that seek to drag me down. I am quite certain you want exactly the same thing for yourself. I have become convinced that the Catholic Church's moral teachings are the key to true and lasting happiness. I've seen them work too many times to be a coincidence. The great saints are proof positive that living according to God's moral truths is *the* solution to the countless problems that plague society today. I've seen enough self-inflicted, sin-induced human sorrow and distress to know that when we ignore or flout God's moral laws, the inevitable result is slavery to vice and addiction, misery, and death. But those who strive by God's grace to adhere to these moral teachings will be following the path that leads inexorably to life, happiness, and freedom.

So to everyone who asks, "Why be Catholic?" I answer, because in the Catholic Church you will receive everything in its fullness that God desires to give you to make you happy and free.

# Notes

## 1. Catholics: The Good, the Bad, and the Ugly

1. http://www.vatican.va/news_services/liturgy/2005/via_crucis/en/station_09.html.

2. Archbishop Seán Patrick O'Malley, 07/30/2003 homily text at his installation Mass, "To those victims . . . we beg forgiveness" (*Boston Globe*, http://www.boston.com/news/packages/omalley/stories/073103_text.htm).

3. Saint Thomas points out that Noah's drunkenness was "without sin" because he did not realize just how strong the wine was that he had vinted and consumed; see *Summa Theologiæ* 2—2ae, q. 150, a. 1.

4. God saved them, though; see Gen. 16:7–15 for the details.

## 2. You *Can* Handle the Truth: The Historical Case for the Catholic Church

1. I.e., renounced their belief in Christ, the "total repudiation of the Christian faith" (*Catechism of the Catholic Church*, para. 2089).

2. In December 1999, the International Theological Commission, with the express approval of then Cardinal Joseph Ratzinger, now Pope Emeritus Benedict XVI, released the document *Memory and Reconciliation: The Church and the Faults of the Past* as a way to both

forthrightly express sorrow and contrition for the sins of Catholics in bygone eras, as well as to set the record straight where necessary. Quoting Pope John Paul II, the commission said, "The purification of memory is thus 'an act of courage and humility in recognizing the wrongs done by those who have borne or bear the name of Christian.' It is based on the conviction that because of 'the bond which unites us to one another in the Mystical Body, all of us, though not personally responsible and without encroaching on the judgement of God, who alone knows every heart, bear the burden of the errors and faults of those who have gone before us.' John Paul II adds: 'As the successor of Peter, I ask that in this year of mercy the Church, strong in the holiness which she receives from her Lord, should kneel before God and implore forgiveness for the past and present sins of her sons and daughters.'"

3. Recent scholarly studies have documented the existence of thousands of separate Protestant denominations. See, for example, Craig D. Atwood, *Handbook of Denominations in the United States* (Nashville: Abingdon Press, 1951–2005, 12th ed.), and David B. Barrett, *World Christian Encyclopedia: A Comparative Survey of Churches and Religions in the Modern World* (Oxford: Oxford University Press, 2001, 2nd ed., two vols.). Barrett's research indicates that, as of 2001, over *25,000* distinct Protestant denominations and subsidiary paradenominations have proliferated globally.

4. The engine of disunity among Protestants was and is Luther's and Calvin's principle of *sola Scriptura* (that the Bible is the sole, formally sufficient rule of faith for the Church). I will expand on this point a little later. For a more in-depth critique of *sola Scriptura* see my book *Scripture and Tradition in the Church: Yves Congar O.P.'s Theology of Revelation and Critique of the Protestant Principle of Sola Scriptura* (Melbourne, Australia: Freedom Publishing, 2014).

5. See the 1964 Vatican II document *Unitatis Redintegratio* ("The Restoration of Unity"), whose opening statement reads, "The restoration of unity among all Christians is one of the principal concerns of the Second Vatican Council. Christ the Lord founded one Church and one Church only. However, many Christian communions present themselves to men as the true inheritors of Jesus

Christ; all indeed profess to be followers of the Lord but differ in mind and go their different ways, as if Christ Himself were divided [1 Cor. 1:13]. Such division openly contradicts the will of Christ, scandalizes the world, and damages the holy cause of preaching the Gospel to every creature."

6. Contrary to what some might imagine, the Second Vatican Council did not "do away with" the Catholic Church's perennial teaching on this point. For example, its document *Lumen Gentium* ("[Christ Is] the Light of the Nations") said: "Basing itself upon Sacred Scripture and Tradition, it teaches that the Church, now sojourning on earth as an exile, is necessary for salvation. Christ, present to us in His Body, which is the Church, is the one Mediator and the unique way of salvation. In explicit terms He Himself affirmed the necessity of faith and baptism [Mark 6:16; John 3:45] and thereby affirmed also the necessity of the Church, for through baptism as through a door men enter the Church. Whosoever, therefore, knowing that the Catholic Church was made necessary by Christ, would refuse to enter or to remain in it, could not be saved" (chap. 14).

7. John Henry Newman, *An Essay on the Development of Christian Doctrine,* p. 7. His conclusion is equally sharp: "This utter incongruity between Protestantism and historical Christianity is a plain fact, whether the latter be regarded in its earlier or in its later centuries. Protestants can as little bear its Ante-Nicene as its Post-Tridentine period" (ibid.).

8. I detail the evidence that supports this claim in my book *Why Is That in Tradition?* (Huntington, IN: Our Sunday Visitor, 2002).

### 3. Brought to My Senses: The Seven Sacraments

1. That is, original sin and all actual sins (one's own personal sins).

2. It is true that all the sacraments nourish the soul with grace, but the Holy Eucharist does so in a particular way in that it involves our eating the Body, Blood, Soul, and Divinity of the glorified, resurrected Jesus Christ, under the appearances of bread and wine.

3. Peter Kreeft and Ronald Tacelli, S.J., use the analogy of a car and

the ocean to show how apologetics (i.e., giving rational reasons for belief in God, Jesus Christ, and so on) is often a necessary precursor for someone to have faith.

4. In Catholic parlance, terms such as "soldier of Christ" are always meant in a nonviolent sense. As Saint Paul said, every Christian should see himself or herself as a soldier of Christ in the sense that they are not "contending against flesh and blood, but against the principalities, against the powers, against the world rulers of this present darkness [i.e., Satan and the fallen angels], against the spiritual hosts of wickedness" (Eph. 6:12).

5. *Catechism of the Catholic Church,* para. 1127.

6. Ibid., para. 1128.

7. St. Thomas Aquinas, *Summa Theologiae,* III. Q.68, 8.

8. Mark Shea, "Why Bother with Such a Corrupt Church?" *National Catholic Register,* August 26, 2012, http://bit.ly/PmkRpX.

9. "In Roman legal language the word *sacramentum* means a pledge deposited in the temple by disputing parties [i.e., a kind of surety bond placed in escrow]" (Ludwig Ott, *Fundamentals of Catholic Dogma* [Charlotte, NC: TAN Books, 1960], p. 325).

10. Augustine, *Epistle* 187, 11:34.

11. *Catechism of the Catholic Church,* para. 774.

12. Although Christ instituted the sacraments, he did not, generally speaking, lay down precise directives regarding how they are to be celebrated. This he left to the authority of the Church, such as when he declared, "Whatever you bind on earth shall be bound in heaven, and whatever you loose on earth shall be loosed in heaven" (Matt. 18:18).

13. It was also known by the name "mystical chrism" in the early Church (see Cyril of Jerusalem, *Catechetical Lectures* 21 in Edwin Hamilton Gifford, ed., *The Catichetical Lectures of S. Cyril, Archbishop of Jerusalem, The Nicene and Post-Nicene Fathers,* Philip Schaff and Henry Wace, eds. [Peabody: Hendrickson Publishers, 1995], vol. 7).

14. *Catechism of the Catholic Church,* para. 1285.

15. Dating to the thirteenth century, this Western custom was not from the apostles.

16. See Genesis chapter 3 for all the details.

17. Mark Lowery, *Living the Good Life: What Every Catholic Needs to Know About Moral Issues* (Ann Arbor, MI: Servant Publications, 2003), pp. 123–24.

18. See also Rom. 2:5–13.

19. The power to ordain belongs to those who are consecrated bishops, thus receiving the fullness of the sacrament of holy orders. See the *Catechism of the Catholic Church,* para. 1554.

20. Circa 1391–1271 B.C.

21. His exhortation for us to imitate him applies not only to imitating his virtue and way of life but also his desire to be thought of and called "father" by his spiritual sons and daughters. This is an important biblical monument manifesting the ancient custom of Catholics calling priests "father," which stretches back to the time of the apostles.

## 4. Soul Food: Mass and the Holy Eucharist

1. Unless a crucifix could be considered a logo.

2. In *The Hidden Manna: A Theology of the Eucharist* (San Francisco: Ignatius Press, 1988), James T. O'Connor says that "St. Ambrose (circa 335–397) . . . may well be the first to refer to the Eucharistic Mystery as 'the Mass'" (p. 38).

3. Luke 22:14–20; see also Matt. 26:26–28 and 1 Cor. 11:23–32.

4. Ignatius of Antioch, *Letter to the Smyrnaeans* 6:2–7:1.

5. Justin Martyr, *First Apology* 66.

6. Irenaeus, *Against Heresies* 4:32–33 and 5:2.

7. Clement of Alexandria, *The Instructor of Children* 1:6. See O'Connor, *The Hidden Manna,* for a survey of the Eucharistic teachings of these and other major patristic witnesses to the Mass and the Eucharist.

8. It was first used formally at the Fourth Lateran Council in 1215.

9. An example commonly used to illustrate this point.

10. This is why, notwithstanding the pious optimism that inhabits the minds of some good and devout Catholics, germs can be communicated at Communion.

11. James T. O'Connor demonstrates in *The Hidden Manna* that both the concept and the term "transubstantiation" were part of

Catholic teaching before it was formally adopted by the Fourth Lateran Council (see pp. 115–121).

12. New American Bible, hereafter NAB.

13. For example, that at the time of consecration during the Mass, Christ becomes truly present, body, blood, soul, and divinity, under the appearances of bread and wine. See *Catechism of the Catholic Church,* paras. 1373–81.

14. "Chick tracts" are so named because they are authored and illustrated by Jack T. Chick (born 1924), an American Fundamentalist Protestant who has made a long and lucrative career out of publishing "evangelistic" booklets and comic books, many of which, like "The Death Cookie," are blatantly anti-Catholic. Chick estimates he has printed and distributed in excess of 800 *million* such tracts in over a dozen languages.

15. A bit of faux Latin doggerel intended to mock the Latin words of consecration at the Mass, where the priest says, "*Hic est enim corpus meum*" ("This is my body").

16. Ignatius himself was torn apart by wild animals at the Colosseum in Rome.

17. Interestingly, the blood is the same type as that found in the Shroud of Turin.

18. In the Mormon Church, a stake center is the equivalent of a Catholic parish. The geographical boundaries of a stake center encompass several "wards," i.e., the smallest unit of membership in a given locality. Local Mormon leaders at the ward level are designated as "bishops," and "stake presidents" supervise stake centers.

19. One of them was his (oddly belated) discovery of the Mormon Church's teaching that abortion, while being a terrible sin, is permissible "in cases of rape and incest." He realized that the Mormon Church could not be the true Church if it could teach such an obviously false notion: that there could ever be a situation in which it is morally justifiable to kill an innocent human being.

## 5. The Cure for What Ails Me: Confession and Healing

1. The *Catechism of the Catholic Church* (para. 1449) says: "The formula of absolution used in the Latin Church expresses the es-

sential elements of this sacrament: the Father of mercies is the source of all forgiveness. He effects the reconciliation of sinners through the Passover of his Son and the gift of his Spirit, through the prayer and ministry of the Church: 'God, the Father of mercies, through the death and the resurrection of his Son has reconciled the world to himself and sent the Holy Spirit among us for the forgiveness of sins; through the ministry of the Church may God give you pardon and peace, and I absolve you from your sins in the name of the Father, and of the Son and of the Holy Spirit.' "

## 6. A Rock That Will Not Roll: Peter and the Papacy

1. Eusebius, *The History of the Church*, bk. 2, chap. 25.
2. Ibid., chap. 14.
3. As foretold by Christ in John 21:18–19: "Truly, truly, I say to you, when you were young, you girded yourself and walked where you would; but when you are old, you will stretch out your hands, and another will gird you and carry you where you do not wish to go. (This he said to show by what death he was to glorify God.) And after this he said to him, 'Follow me.' "
4. See J. N. D. Kelly, *The Oxford Dictionary of Popes* (Oxford: Oxford University Press, 1986), and Warren H. Carroll, *The Founding of Christendom* (Front Royal, VA: Christendom Publications, 1985), pp. 447–559.
5. In Hebrew, Simon is pronounced "Shemón," and means "He [i.e., God] has heard." The Greek name Simon was also well known.
6. Cephas is the Greek transliteration of the Aramaic word *kepha*.
7. See, for example, Luke 9:32; Acts 2:37 and 5:29; and John 18:15 and 20:2–4.
8. Matt. 10:2–4; Mark 3:14—19; Luke 6:13–16; and Acts 1:13.
9. Saint John, writing for a Greek-speaking audience, preserved two non-Greek words from this exchange between Jesus and Peter. The first is the Hebrew word "messiah," which, in his parenthetical comment, he translates into Greek as *christos;* the second is the Aramaic word *kepha,* meaning "rock," which he translates into Greek as *petros.*
10. Also rendered as "Symeon" (see Acts 15:14 and 2 Peter 1:1).

11. This notion has been thoroughly debunked by the Protestant Scripture scholar Oscar Cullmann in Gerhard Kittel and Gerhard Friedrich, eds., *Theological Dictionary of the New Testament* (Grand Rapids, MI: Wm. B. Eerdmans, 1968), vol. 6, pp. 95–108.

12. The Lord's words to Simon Peter in Matthew 16 are strikingly reminiscent of what God said about Israel's prime minister in Isa. 22:15–25.

13. "Barque" and its variant, "bark," are archaic terms for a sailing ship.

14. See also Mark 14:29–31; Luke 22:33–34; and John 13:36–38.

15. For a representative series of notable patristic quotations that demonstrate this point, see my book *Why Is That in Tradition?* (Huntington, IN: Our Sunday Visitor, 2002), pp. 43–60. See also Scott Butler, Norman Dahlgren, and David Hess, *Jesus, Peter & the Keys* (Santa Barbara, CA: Queenship Publishing, 1997).

16. Patrick Madrid, *Pope Fiction: Answers to 30 Myths and Misconceptions About the Papacy* (San Diego: Basilica Press, 1999), p. 24.

17. The Vatican I (1870) document *Pastor Aeternus* (*Eternal Shepherd*) outlines the specific parameters of this doctrine as they pertain both to the magisterium, or teaching office of the Catholic Church (i.e., the bishops), and to the pope.

18. Twenty-one such councils have taken place during the life span of the Catholic Church, the first one being the First Council of Nicaea (325) and the last one being Vatican II (1962–1965).

19. Madrid, *Pope Fiction*, pp. 138–39.

20. For my response to that argument, see ibid., pp. 37–50.

21. Matt. 14:31 and 28:17; John 20:24–28.

22. John 6:66–71.

23. Luke 9:46.

24. Luke 9:51–56.

25. The San Diego–based, lay-run Catholic apologetics organization where I worked for eight years, from January 1988 to January 1996.

26. For an aggregation of articles detailing this incident, enter "Bojinka Bomb Plot" in the search engine of the *New York Times*' website, topics.nytimes.com.

27. Jonathon and I made it safely home, too, though only after a

nerve-racking bomb scare in Osaka, Japan, where we had a two-hour layover before our connecting flight to Los Angeles. Airport authorities in Osaka explained that a credible bomb threat had been made against our flight, and they needed to remove and rescreen all the luggage before allowing us to reboard. We also learned that every single seat in the 747-400 aircraft was removed and inspected for concealed bombs and that bomb-sniffing dogs made a sweep through it as well. I vividly recall how, when we finally boarded the plane, hours after our originally scheduled departure time, I experienced a strange mixture of emotions: apprehension because of the bomb threat and relief at knowing the plane had been so thoroughly checked over by security. One final, bizarre twist to that day was the terrible coincidence that unfolded only a few hours after our plane departed Osaka—a devastating 6.8 magnitude earthquake struck the City of Kobe, just a few miles across Osaka Bay from where we had been standing in Kansai Airport. Nearly sixty-five hundred people were killed in the quake, which happened while our flight was in the air headed for LAX. Ours was the first flight to arrive in Los Angeles after the quake, and the first inkling we had that something bad had happened was (once again) a throng of television news cameras clustered around our arrival gate, with reporters interviewing disembarking passengers shocked by the unexpected news of the earthquake. That was the second—and I hope the *last*—time in my life I have been present at such an eerie scene.

28. For thorough documentation of this issue, see Stéphane Courtois et al., *The Black Book of Communism: Crimes, Terror, Repression* (Cambridge, MA: Harvard University Press, 1999), pp. 408–23. See also Associated Press, "Kremlin Targeted Pope, Ex-KGB Official Says," *Los Angeles Times,* March 2, 1990.

29. While the location of Saint Peter's martyrdom is known (Nero's Circus on Vatican Hill), the exact date remains unclear: between A.D. 64 and 67.

30. For details, see Carroll, *Founding of Christendom,* and Kelly, *Oxford Dictionary of Popes.*

31. A.D. 130–202.

32. Irenaeus, *Against Heresies,* 3:3., emphasis mine.

33. The epistle is commonly thought to have been composed around A.D. 95, though there is convincing evidence to support a date as early as 70. For a detailed analysis of the evidence, see Rev. Thomas J. Herron, *Clement and the Early Church of Rome: On the Dating of Clement's First Epistle to the Corinthians* (Steubenville, OH: Emmaus Road Publishing, 2010).

34. Clement, *Epistle to the Corinthians,* 59.

35. Ibid., 63.

36. John Chapman, "Clement I, Saint, Pope," *The Catholic Encyclopedia* (New York: Robert Appleton, 1908), vol. 4, pp. 12–17.

37. Three books that chronicle the calamitous decades after Vatican II, though from very different ideological perspectives, are Peter Steinfels, *A People Adrift: The Crisis of the Roman Catholic Church in America* (New York: Simon & Schuster, 2004); George A. Kelly, *The Battle for the American Church* (New York: Doubleday, 1981); and Russell Shaw, *American Church: The Remarkable Rise, Meteoric Fall, and Uncertain Future of Catholicism in America* (San Francisco: Ignatius Press, 2013).

38. In *Witness to Hope: The Biography of Pope John Paul II* (New York: HarperCollins, 1999), George Weigel provides a sweeping and meticulously detailed account of John Paul II's papacy.

## 7. Mamma Mia!: The Blessed Virgin Mary's Role in God's Plan of Salvation

1. Jean-Michel Coulet, ed., *An Invitation to Faith: An A to Z Primer on the Thought of Pope Benedict XVI* (San Francisco: Ignatius Press, 2007).

2. The Hebrew word for "bruise" here is "shuwph," also translated as "crush" or "fall upon."

3. William A. Jurgens, *The Faith of the Early Fathers,* 3 vols. (Collegeville, MN: Liturgical Press, 1970).

4. Hilda Graef, *Mary: A History of Doctrine and Devotion* (London: Sheed & Ward, 1963).

5. Luigi Gambero, *Mary and the Fathers of the Church* (San Francisco: Ignatius Press, 1999). See also Luigi Gambero, *Mary in the Mid-*

*dle Ages* (San Francisco: Ignatius Press, 2005); George H. Tavard, *The Thousand Faces of the Virgin Mary* (Collegeville, MN: Liturgical Press, 1996); and Jaroslav Pelikan, *Mary Through the Centuries* (New Haven, CT: Yale University Press, 1996).

6. *Catechism of the Catholic Church,* paras. 967–68.

7. See Rom. 12:4–5; 1 Cor. 12:12–30.

8. I recall how impressed I was upon learning of Saint Dominic Savio's motto, "Death before sin!" I chose Dominic as my confirmation name, and prayed to him countless times in my youth, asking for his intercession as I fought (and often lost) my own battles with purity and chastity as a teenager and young man. None of which is to suggest any deficiency on his part! In fact, I believe that, by God's grace, Saint Dominic's prayerful intercession, and that of the Blessed Virgin Mary, prevented me from sliding much further downward toward the precipice.

9. John Paul II, *Rosarium Virginis Mariae,* 2002.

10. For a fuller discussion of the issue of repetitious prayer, see my books *Answer Me This!* (Huntington, IN: Our Sunday Visitor, 2003), pp. 146–48, and *Does the Bible Really Say That?: Discovering Catholic Teaching in Scripture* (Cincinnati: Servant Books, 2006), pp. 62–64.

11. Juan Diego (1474–1548) is now a canonized saint. His original name was *Cuauhtlatoatzin.*

12. Keep in mind that this discourse, which may seem strange to us today, was framed in language that a simple peasant would readily understand. Mary identified herself as the "Mother of God," not in the sense that she somehow "predated" God (an impossibility, since she is a finite creature), but in the sense given by the First Council of Ephesus (A.D. 431), which declared Christ's mother, Mary, to be the *theotókos* (Greek for "God-Bearer," which in Latin is translated as *Mater Dei*—"Mother of God"). Because Mary gave birth to Christ, both God and man, a Divine Person, she is known as the Mother of God.

13. Known in the Nahuatl language as *Nican Mopohua,* this account of the apparitions is generally attributed to Bernardino de Sahagún (1499–1590), a Spanish scholar of the Nahuatl language

and culture, and his research assistant Antonio Valeriano (1531–1605). See Miguel León-Portilla, *Bernardino de Sahagún: First Anthropologist* (Norman: University of Oklahoma Press, 2002).

14. For the details, see my presentation "Viva Cristo Rey! The Persecution of the Catholic Church in Mexico in the 1920s" (available in CD, DVD, and MP3 formats at http://www.patrickmadrid.com).

15. For a detailed study of the phenomenon of the image on the *tilma* and the history of the Guadalupe apparitions, see Warren H. Carroll, *Our Lady of Guadalupe: And the Conquest of Darkness* (Front Royal, VA: Christendom Press, 2004), and Carl Anderson, *Our Lady of Guadalupe: Mother of the Civilization of Love* (New York: Doubleday Religion, 2009).

16. See 1 Pet. 3:21.

17. God said to Moses: "The blood shall be a sign for you, upon the houses where you are; and when I see the blood, I will pass over you, and no plague shall fall upon you to destroy you, when I smite the land of Egypt" (Exod. 12:13).

## 8. How 'bout Them Saints?: Mystics, Martyrs, and Miracle-Workers

1. Thomas J. Craughwell, *Saints Behaving Badly* (New York: Doubleday, 2006).

2. A dualistic religion originating in Persia that "purported to be the true synthesis of all the religious systems then known, and actually consisted of Zoroastrian Dualism, Babylonian folklore, Buddhist ethics, and some small and superficial additions of Christian elements. . . . [It taught the] theory of two eternal principles, good and evil [and promised] salvation by knowledge. Manichaeism professed to be a religion of pure reason as opposed to Christian credulity; it professed to explain the origin, the composition, and the future of the universe; it had an answer for everything and despised Christianity" (J. Arendzen, *The Catholic Encyclopedia* [New York: Robert Appleton, 1910], vol. 4, p. 59).

3. Augustine, *Confessions* bk. 9, chap. 1.

4. Saint Stephen, the Church's first martyr, went straight to heaven as a result of his supreme sacrifice (Acts 7; see also Matt. 10:32,

39, and 16:25). This exemplifies the traditional view in Catholicism regarding those who die for Christ, as expressed by Saint Augustine: "It is an affront to a martyr to pray for him; we should rather recommend ourselves to *his* prayers (*Sermon* 159:1; emphasis added).

5. He was the founder of the Salesian religious order of priests, named in honor of Saint Francis de Sales (1567–1622). For background on Saint Francis de Sales and his uncanny ability to make converts to the Catholic Church, see my book *On a Mission: Lessons from St. Francis de Sales* (Cincinnati: Servant Books, 2013).

6. For a detailed account of this bloody persecution of the Church in Mexico in the 1920s, see my lecture "Attack on Religious Liberty: Battle for the Faith in Mexico," available in English and Spanish at http://www.lighthousecatholicmedia.com. See also Francis Clement Kelley, *Blood-Drenched Altars* (Charlotte, NC: TAN Books, 2009); Wilfrid Parsons, *Mexican Martyrdom* (Charlotte, NC: TAN Books, 2009); and Ann Ball, *Blessed Miguel Pro: 20th-Century Mexican Martyr* (Charlotte, NC: TAN Books, 2009).

7. "Blessed Miguel Agustín Pro," http://www.americancatholic.org.

8. For an astonishing catalog of such examples, see Herbert J. Thurston, S.J., ed., *Butler's Lives of the Saints: Complete Edition,* 4 vols. (Allen, TX: Christian Classics, 1996); Brian O'Neel, *Saint Who? 39 Holy Unknowns* (Cincinnati: Servant Books, 2012); and Elizabeth Ficocelli, *Bleeding Hands, Weeping Stone: True Stories of Divine Wonders, Miracles, and Messages* (Charlotte, NC: Saint Benedict Press, 2010).

9. John Paul II, apostolic letter, *Divini Amoris Scientia (Saint Thérèse of the Child Jesus and the Holy Face Is Proclaimed a Doctor of the Universal Church),* October 19, 1997.

10. Thomas à Kempis (1380–1471) was not canonized, but *The Imitation of Christ* rightly ranks among the greatest Christian writings on the spiritual life ever.

11. Chesterton (1874–1936) and Sheen (1895–1979) are also not yet canonized saints. Sheen's cause for canonization has been under way for some years now; go to http://www.archbishopsheencause.org.

12. The Eternal Word Television Network (EWTN) has a helpful

overview of this process at http://www.ewtn.com/johnpaul2/cause/process.asp. The *Catechism of the Catholic Church* (paras. 960–62) explains the Communion of Saints as follows: "The Church is a 'communion of saints': this expression refers first to the 'holy things' *(sancta)*, above all the Eucharist, by which 'the unity of believers, who form one body in Christ, is both represented and brought about' *(Lumen Gentium, 3)*. The term 'communion of saints' refers also to the communion of 'holy persons' *(sancti)* in Christ who 'died for all,' so that what each one does or suffers in and for Christ bears fruit for all. 'We believe in the communion of all the faithful of Christ, those who are pilgrims on earth, the dead who are being purified, and the blessed in heaven, all together forming one Church; and we believe that in this communion, the merciful love of God and his saints is always [attentive] to our prayers'" (Paul VI, CPG § 30).

13. In every conversation that I've had with Bible-believing Christians (Catholics and Protestants), and with whom I've followed this sequence of biblical truths, none has ever disagreed with any of the four, which makes it very difficult to honestly disagree with the conclusion I believe one must draw from them.

14. See also Gal. 3:28; Eph. 1:22–23 and 5:21–32; Col. 1:18 and 3:15; and Heb. 13:1–3.

15. George J. Marlin, et al., eds., *The Quotable Chesterton: A Topical Compilation of the Wit, Wisdom and Satire of G.K. Chesterton* (San Francisco: Ignatius Press, 1986).

16. Revelation depicts the saints and angels in heaven as intercessors, presenting the prayers of the "holy ones" on earth as bowls of incense (see Rev. 5:6–8 and 8:3–4).

## 9. Hello, I Love You: The Catholic Church's Charitable Good Works

1. For more information on the Pontifical Council Cor Unum, go to http://www.corunum.va.

2. For a comprehensive look at the history of Catholic hospitals and health care, from the early Church to the early twentieth century,

see James Joseph Walsh, "Hospitals," *The Catholic Encyclopedia* (New York: Robert Appleton, 1910), vol. 7, pp. 480–88.

3. See also Deut. 27:19; Ps. 10:14; Prov. 23:9–11; Isa. 1:17; and Zech. 7:9–11.

4. Plato observed that the elderly are "very wroth with those who despitefully entreat orphans and waifs, regarding these as a trust most solemn and sacred. To all these authorities the guardian and official—if he has a spark of sense—must pay attention; he must show as much care regarding the nurture and training of the orphans as if he were contributing to his own support and that of his own children, and he must do them good in every way to the utmost of his power" (*Laws* 927a–b).

5. Lactantius (c. 240–320), *The Divine Institutes* 6:12. In this passage, Lactantius also underscores the priority the Church placed on hospitality, ransoming prisoners, welcoming strangers, and burying the dead.

6. See Antoine Dégert, "St. Vincent de Paul," *The Catholic Encyclopedia* (New York: Robert Appleton, 1912), vol. 15, pp. 434–37.

7. Ibid., p. 437.

8. For a historical account of these legendary Jesuit missions, portrayed beautifully (though, in some respects, inaccurately) in Roland Joffé's 1986 film *The Mission,* see Philip Caraman, *The Lost Paradise: The Jesuit Republic in South America* (London: Sidgwick & Jackson, 1975). See also my book *Pope Fiction: Answers to 30 Myths and Misconceptions About the Papacy* (San Diego: Basilica Press, 1999), pp. 199–219.

9. For a detailed contemporary chronicle of these missions to the Indians, see Reuben Gold Thwaites, ed., *The Jesuit Relations and Allied Documents: Travels and Explorations of the Jesuit Missionaries in New France, 1610–1791,* http://puffin.creighton.edu/jesuit/relations/relations_01.html (71 vols.).

10. Mother Teresa's religious order, the Missionaries of Charity, continues these charitable good works around the world, working almost exclusively in the poorest regions.

11. William Doino Jr., "Mother Teresa and Her Critics," *First Things,* April 1, 2013, http://www.firstthings.com/onthesquare/2013/04/mother-teresa-and-her-critics.

12. Thomas E. Woods Jr., *How the Catholic Church Built Western Civilization* (Washington, DC: Regnery, 2012), pp. 43–44.
13. Quoted in ibid., p. 47.
14. That is, "charity," in biblical terms (see 1 Cor. 13).
15. For recent statistics on the scope of Catholic charitable service to the poor and needy in America, see *Forbes*, "The 200 Largest U.S. Charities," http://www.forbes.com/lists/2005/14/Revenue_1 .html. Note that the aggregate of all Catholic organizations on this list (e.g., Catholic Charities, Catholic Medical Mission Board, Catholic Relief Services, Covenant House, etc.) reflects a significant portion of the total financial picture that emerges from these statistics.

## 10. Ah, the Good Life: The Awe, Wonder, and Goodness of God

1. See, for example, Régine Pernoud, *Those Terrible Middle Ages: Debunking the Myths* (San Francisco: Ignatius Press, 2000); Thomas E. Woods Jr., *How the Catholic Church Built Western Civilization* (Washington, DC: Regnery, 2012); and Diane Moczar, *Seven Lies About Catholic History* (Charlotte, NC: Saint Benedict Press, 2012).
2. For an overview, see the chapter on Galileo in my book *Pope Fiction: Answers to 30 Myths and Misconceptions About the Papacy* (San Diego: Basilica Press, 1999), pp. 178–89.
3. See http://www.magisreasonfaith.org for more about Father Spitzer's innovative work demonstrating the unity and complementarity of faith and science.
4. John Paul II, *Fides et Ratio,* paras. 69, 106, http://www.vatican.va. As Régine Pernoud points out in *Those Terrible Middle Ages: Debunking the Myths*.
5. Robert Sokolowski, *Introduction to Phenomenology* (Cambridge: Cambridge University Press, 2000), p. 2.
6. Ibid., p. 46.
7. The U.S. Treasury Department's website, www.treasury.gov, reports the debt at just over $16.7 trillion.
8. NASA reports that, in 2011, the Hubble Space Telescope spotted Galaxy MACS0647-JD at a distance of 13.3 *billion* light-years.

9. "Oh Great God," composed by the Swedish Protestant poet Carl Gustav Boberg (1859–1940).

10. Dan Lord, *Choosing Joy* (Huntington, IN: Our Sunday Visitor, 2012), p. 19.

11. *Catechism of the Catholic Church,* para. 1749.

12. In fact, "missiology" is a branch of Catholic theology that "studies the principles and practice of the missions. It is the science of evangelization and catechesis in regions and among people where the Church is being established" (John A. Hardon, S.J., *Modern Catholic Dictionary* [Bardstown, KY: Eternal Life Publications, 2000]).

13. Jesus clarifies his meaning, saying, "Truly, truly, I say to you, unless one is born *of water and the Spirit,* he cannot enter the kingdom of God (emphasis added)" (John 3:5). After his discussion with Nicodemus, we are told that Jesus and his disciples "went into the land of Judea, [and] there he remained with them and baptized" (John 3:22). Numerous other New Testament passages attest to the regenerating and saving effects of the sacrament of baptism (e.g., see Acts 2:38 and 22:16; Rom. 6:1–4; Eph. 5:25–27; Col. 2:12–13; Titus 3:5; 1 Pet. 3:18–22).

14. J. M. Lehen, trans., *Confessions of Saint Augustine* (Totowa, NJ: Catholic Book Publishing Company, 1997), 1:1.

15. http://cara.georgetown.edu/CARAServices/requestedchurch stats.html.

16. Ibid.

17. I won't try to explain the causes of this implosion of religious vocations among American Catholic women, but for those who are interested, plausible explanations are given in books such as Donna Steichen, *Ungodly Rage: The Hidden Face of Catholic Feminism* (San Francisco: Ignatius Press, 1991), and Rosemary Keefe Curb and Nancy Manahan, *Lesbian Nuns: Breaking Silence* (Tallahassee, FL: Naiad Press, 1985). (Keefe Curb is an ex-nun and Manahan is a lesbian.) See also the heartbreaking interview with Dr. William Coulson, a psychologist who is a disciple of Abraham Maslow and a colleague of Carl Rogers, entitled "We Overcame Their Traditions, We Overcame Their Faith," http://www.ewtn.com/library/priests/coulson.txt. In it he explains exactly how he and Rogers employed a technique called nondirective therapy, which resulted

in the demolition of a religious order known as the Sisters of the Immaculate Heart of Mary.

18. Ann Carey, "The CARA Study and Vocations," *Catholic World Report,* May 7, 2011.

19. Vatican II, *Gaudium et Spes,* para. 50, sec. 1; see also Gen. 2:18; Matt. 19:4; and Gen. 1:28.

20. For an eye-opening catalog of controversial statements by Planned Parenthood officials, see http://www.ewtn.com/library/prolenc/encyc067.htm.

21. "Contraception: Why Not?," http://www.catholiceducation.org.

22. The major exceptions are child pornography and pornography depicting bestiality.

23. Victor Hugo, *Les Misérables.*

24. C. S. Lewis, *The Great Divorce,* chap. 11.

# Acknowledgments

My sincere thanks go to everyone on the Random House–Image team who were involved with the production of this book, especially Gary Jansen, for seeking me out in the first place and inviting me to write it, and Amanda O'Connor, my ace editor, who persistently and skillfully helped me burnish my original manuscript into something even better.

I am especially thankful to Cardinal Seán Patrick O'Malley, O.F.M. Cap., for his generosity in taking time out of his preternaturally busy schedule to compose the gracious foreword for this book.

And I am deeply grateful for my wife, Nancy, and her patient, loving support (especially when I hunker down into book-writing mode), and all the others in my life who have shown me by their good example and encouragement what it means to be Catholic, especially in how they exemplify the goodness and virtue that come from striving to love God with all one's heart, soul, and mind.

Thank you all. May God reward you.

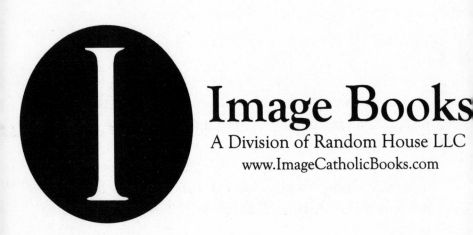

# Image Books

A Division of Random House LLC

www.ImageCatholicBooks.com

## Publishing Books of Catholic Interest Since 1954

Bible Study • Biography/Memoir • Family • Formation
Inspirational • Saints • Reference • Spirituality • Theology